Getting Started with
TypeScript

Thomas Claudius Huber

1st Edition, February 2017
Copyright © 2017 by Thomas Claudius Huber
All rights reserved

Author: Thomas Claudius Huber
Layout: Thomas Claudius Huber
Cover: Julia Huber and www.juhu-design.com

ISBN-13: 978-1539943587
ISBN-10: 1539943585

No part of this book may be stored, reproduced or transmitted in any form or by any means without express written permission of the author.

For my 4 girls
Julia, Anna, Sara & Elsa
♥

Chapter Overview

1. Introduction 11
2. Setting up Your Environment 21
3. Using TypeScript 25
4. Basic Types... 41
5. Var, Let and Const 61
6. Interfaces and Classes 65
7. Generics 85
8. Functions 93
9. Modules 107
10. Decorators.. 125
11. Declaration Files 135
12. Angular with TypeScript 143
Index 173

Table of Contents

1. **Introduction** 11
    Welcome! 11
    Is this Book for You? 11
    About JavaScript and ECMA 12
    JavaScript for Enterprise Apps 13
    The Power of TypeScript 14
    Structure of this Book 15
    Getting the Samples 16
    Run the Samples 17
    Feedback 17
    About the Author 18
2. **Setting up Your Environment** 21
    Introduction 21
    Install Node.js and NPM 21
    Install TypeScript 22
    Install Visual Studio Code 23
    Install Google Chrome 24
    Summary 24
3. **Using TypeScript** 25
    Introduction 25
    Run a Simple, Buggy JavaScript File 25
    Introduce TypeScript 28
    Add and Use an Interface 29
    Fix the Code 30
    Define Compiler Options 31
    Create and Use a tsconfig.json-file 33
    Debug your TypeScript Code 35
    Hide JS in Visual Studio Code 37
    Summary 39
4. **Basic Types** 41
    Introduction 41
    Boolean 41

Type Inference 42
Number.. 43
String 44
Arrays 46
Iterating Arrays: for...of and for...in 47
For... in on Objects.. 48
Tuples 49
Enums... 49
The any type 51
Type Assertions 53
Union Types 55
Returning Void 57
Never.. 57
Undefined, null and Strict Null Checking 58
Summary 59

5. Var, Let and Const 61
Introduction 61
Declare Variables 61
Function-scoped vs. Block-scoped... 61
Multiple Declarations 62
Declare Before Access 63
Using Const 64
Summary 64

6. Interfaces and Classes 65
Introduction 65
Interfaces.. 65
Create and Instantiate a Class... 67
Implement an Interface.. 70
Type Compatibility in TypeScript 70
Access Modifiers of Class Members.. 71
Parameter Properties.. 72
Readonly Properties 73
Properties with Accessors.. 75
Static Properties... 76
Inheritance 77

Abstract Classes	78
Constructor Parameters	79
The instanceof Operator	80
Destructuring Objects	81
Summary	83

7. Generics 85
Introduction	85
The Generic Array Type	85
Generic Functions	86
Generic Interfaces	87
Generic Classes	88
Generic Constraints	89
Multiple Type Parameters	91
Summary	92

8. Functions 93
Introduction	93
Types of Functions in JavaScript	93
Adding Types to Functions	94
Optional Parameters	94
Default Values	95
Rest Parameters	96
Functions as Parameters	97
Interfaces for Functions	98
Functions and This	99
Arrow Functions	101
Async and Await	103
Summary	105

9. Modules 107
Introduction	107
Module Basics	107
Export and Import	108
Setting Up a Module Loader	109
How to Install Dependencies for a Project	117
Export Multiple Types	117
Import Multiple Types	118

Use Export Aliases 119
Use Import Aliases 120
Default Export 120
Exporting Variables and Functions 121
Summary 123

10. Decorators 125
Introduction 125
Decorator Basics 125
Turn on Decorator Support 126
Create a Property Decorator 127
Create a Class Decorator 129
Use the Reflect-metadata Library 131
Component Decorator in Angular 133
Summary 134

11. Declaration Files 135
Introduction 135
Include a Simple JavaScript-library 135
Declare a Function 137
Install Declaration Files from NPM 137
Write Your Own Library with Declarations 139
Summary 141

12. Angular with TypeScript 143
Introduction 143
Run the Angular Book Samples 143
Hello World in Angular 145
Directives in Angular 150
Create Lists with ngFor 150
Display Details with ngIf 154
Data Binding in Angular 155
Add a Two-Way Data Binding 156
Create a Friend Component 157
Connect to GitHub via Http 161
Extract Http-logic into a Service 167
Summary 170

Index 173

1. Introduction

Welcome!

Hi! Thanks for picking up the book "Getting Started with TypeScript". This book has been written to introduce you into the TypeScript programming language and all its power. TypeScript is a superset of JavaScript that compiles down to plain JavaScript. It gives you static typing and latest JavaScript features.

TypeScript is open source and maintained by Microsoft and C# inventor Anders Hejlsberg. Today it has a broad adoption. For example, Google has written its popular Single Page Application (SPA) framework Angular in TypeScript. Beside TypeScript, this book contains an introduction on how to build modern, component-based web-applications with Angular.

But what does the broad adoption of TypeScript mean for you?

As a serious software developer, TypeScript is a language you should definitely have in your pocket! And as TypeScript is a JavaScript superset that compiles down to plain JavaScript, there are only advantages when you prefer programming in TypeScript over programming in plain JavaScript.

Before you learn about the advantages of TypeScript, about the structure of this book, about the used samples and about how to contact the author, let's check if this book is for you.

Is this Book for You?

This book is about TypeScript, which is a superset of JavaScript. To read this book and to get most out of it, you don't have to have any previous knowledge in JavaScript or TypeScript. Even not in HTML or Web development. We really start from scratch.

But if you see a for-loop or an if-statement, you should be able to read that. I won't discuss very basic things like "what is a variable" and "how do I assign a value to a variable" in this book.

So, if you know the basics of any programming language like C#, C++, Java, JavaScript, PHP etc., then this book is for you! If you know more than the basics, this book is also for you. If you don't know the basics of any programming language, you can try reading this book, but don't say you haven't been warned in this section.

Alright, are you ready? Let's take a quick look at JavaScript.

About JavaScript and ECMA

JavaScript's popularity is exploding. This is because over the past years several great technologies popped up:
- There are popular frameworks to build applications with JavaScript, like React, Angular and many others
- With Node.js you can run server-side JavaScript
- With Electron, you can use JavaScript to build standalone desktop-apps for Windows, Mac OS and Linux
- With Cordova, you can use JavaScript to build mobile apps for iOS and Android
- ...

JavaScript itself is standardized by the *European Computer Manufacturers Association* (ECMA). That's the reason why JavaScript is often called ECMAScript or just ES, like it is used in this book.

Over the past decades, the ECMA has brought out several standards:

1997 – ECMAScript 1
1998 – ECMAScript 2
1999 – ECMAScript 3
2009 – ECMAScript 5

Don't try to polish your glasses. There's no standard missing between ES3 and ES5. An ES4 standard was never released. The ECMA worked on ES4, but it was abandoned due to political differences concerning the features and complexity of the language. After ES5 these are the next standards:

2015 – ECMAScript 2015
2016 – ECMAScript 2016
2017 – ECMAScript 2017

As you can see, the ECMA decided in 2015 to use the year number for all future standardizations instead of a classic integer version number. When you read about the standards, you might still find writings using classic version numbers for the new standards. For example, if you read something about ES6, that means that ES6 is equal to ES2015. ES7 is equal to ES2016 and ES8 is equal to ES2017.

JavaScript for Enterprise Apps

JavaScript is a language that was written in a few weeks. It was built to execute code in websites to adjust content dynamically. And it was invented to write around 100 or maybe up to 1.000 lines of code with it. Nobody expected that developers might use it one day to build large-scale enterprise applications. But today we are at this point: Developers are using JavaScript to write enterprise applications with 100.000 or even more lines of code.

Sure, you can write such large applications with JavaScript, but these big applications are hard to maintain. The reason for hard maintainability is quite often because JavaScript is a dynamic language. Types are not checked at compile time like in a static typed language like C# or Java. And this leads to errors that only appear at runtime. Let's look at a sample.

Let's assume you have this JavaScript code:

```
function logFirstName(friend) {
   console.log(friend.firstName);
}
logFirstName("just a string");
```

Listing 1.1: Simple JavaScript code

The `logFirstName`-function has a `friend`-parameter. The function grabs the `firstName`-property of the passed-in object and logs it to the browser's console. After the function-definition the function is called with a plain string. But a string does not have a `firstName`-property. So, what will happen here?

In JavaScript passing a string to the function from listing 1.1 doesn't lead to a compile-time error. Instead the browser's console will contain the text "undefined", as the `firstName`-property is not available on a string object.

Now imagine a large JavaScript codebase. You might have errors like in listing 1.1. But as your codebase is huge, the errors are not as obvious as in listing 1.1. Beside the errors, documentation is also something that is not so good. Note that you have to look into the body of the `logFirstName`-function to find out that the passed in object needs to have a `firstName`-property. Now what if you have a more complex function that has not just one line in its body? It's not hard to imagine that this is a problem that requires a lot of documentation for the function in JavaScript. Developers are writing comments on top of functions to explain the inputs and outputs, as there's no compile time check.

All these drawbacks show one problem with JavaScript: JavaScript has no static typing. And this is exactly where TypeScript comes in. It brings the static typed parts that make languages like C# and Java very robust to the JavaScript world.

The Power of TypeScript

TypeScript is a superset of JavaScript. That means that any JavaScript code is already valid TypeScript code. Just change the file-extension from *.js* to *.ts* and extend your JavaScript code with types to get compile-time errors. In case of listing 1.1, you can add an interface like shown in listing 1.2. You can use that interface for the `friend`-parameter of the `logFirstName`-function. Now passing in a string when calling that function leads to a compile-time error, as there's no `firstName`-property on a string.

```
interface Friend {
  firstName: string;
}
function logFirstName(friend: Friend) {
  console.log(friend.firstName);
}
logFirstName("just a string"); // Compile-time error
```

Listing 1.2: Types in TypeScript

> **Note**
>
> You'll learn how to compile TypeScript later in this book in chapter 3, "Using TypeScript".

You can fix the error from listing 1.2 by calling the `logFirstName`-function with a correct object that has a `firstName`-property:

```
logFirstName({ firstName : "Thomas" });
```

When you write the above object with the `firstName`-property in an editor like Visual Studio Code, you even get statement completion for the `firstName`-property, as that property is known at compile-time. So, with Typescript, you get not only compile-time errors, but also great tooling support.

The TypeScript code that you write in a *.ts*-file gets compiled to plain JavaScript, so a *.js*-file gets generated. That means that TypeScript is not visible in the deployment of your application. The deployment will be plain JavaScript that was compiled from TypeScript. And this leads - beside the static typing – to another huge advantage of TypeScript over classic JavaScript: You can use the latest JavaScript features today in TypeScript and compile them down to older JavaScript versions that are supported in today's browsers. You learn in chapter 3, "Using TypeScript", how to adjust the target JavaScript version in the TypeScript compiler options.

Let's wrap this up: TypeScript has some big advantages over classic JavaScript:
- static typing, which makes it robust for big applications
- great tooling support, as types are available at compile-time
- compiles latest JavaScript-features to older JavaScript versions that are supported by today's browsers

Structure of this Book

If you don't have any TypeScript knowledge, you'll have the best experience to read this book from start to end. If you have some knowledge, you can jump to individual chapters if you want.

The book starts from scratch: You learn in the next chapter how to set up your environment before we jump into the details of TypeScript. You learn how to change a JavaScript-file to TypeScript, how to use the compiler, how to set compiler options and more. Then you learn in the upcoming chapters of this book about types, var and let, interfaces, classes, functions, decorators, declaration files and at the end even about how TypeScript is used in Angular.

The book is using some formatting styles:

```
This is a -commandline command
```

```
This is an output in the browser's console
```

> **Note**
> This is a note that gives you a hint or explains something more detailed.

```
This is either typescript or javascript code
```

Getting the Samples

The samples of this book are available for download from GitHub:

https://github.com/thomasclaudiushuber/Getting-Started-with-TypeScript

The samples are structured in folders that match the chapter numbers of this book:

- 02 (Setting up Your Environment)
- 03 (Using TypeScript)
- 04 (Basic Types)
- ...

Below a code listing you find the path to the file that contains the code. Listing 3.1 shows for example the content of a *main.js*-file of chapter 3 that is in the folder *03\starter*:

```
function printFirstNames(friends) {
    for (let friend of friends) {
        console.log(friend.firstName);
    }
}
printFirstNames(7);
```

Listing 3.1: *03\starter\main.js*

Run the Samples

The book samples contain two kind of samples:
- Those with a *package.json*-file
- And those without

For those samples with a *package.json*-file, you need to do two steps to run the sample.

Step 1: Install the dependencies defined in the *package.json*-file by going to the command line and call:

```
npm install
```

Npm is the Node Package Manager. You install it in chapter 2, "Setting up Your Environment" and you learn more about the *package.json*-file in chapter 9, "Modules", when you set up a module loader.

Step 2: After you've installed the dependencies, you can call this on the command line:

```
npm start
```

This fires up a web server and the TypeScript compiler. The app runs in the browser. That's it for those samples with a *package.json*-file.

Then there are the other samples without a *package.json*-file. For these samples, you just start the *index.html* from the directory by double-clicking it. You compile the TypeScript code by calling the compiler on the command line with this statement:

```
tsc
```

You install the TypeScript compiler in chapter 2, "Setting up Your Environment" and you learn a lot about the command line and `tsc` in chapter 3, "Using TypeScript".

Feedback

If you have any questions about this book or if you have any feedback how this book could be improved, please reach out to me:

Email: thomas@thomasclaudiushuber.com

Twitter: @thomasclaudiush

About the Author

Thomas Claudius Huber is a Microsoft Most Valuable Professional (MVP) for Windows Development. Thomas loves programming, but he doesn't like to write about himself in a third-person perspective. Let's switch to the first person:

Hi there, I'm Thomas! Let me introduce myself. I love to write code and I love to create professional applications. My main focus is on writing business applications in C# and TypeScript using technologies like Universal Windows Platform, Angular, ASP.NET Core, Node.js and Azure.

I started programming in 2001 with Java before I learned other languages like PL/SQL, PHP, C#, ActionScript or JavaScript. I was always highly interested in and fascinated by architecture and user interfaces. So, after my studies I started elaborating a strong expertise in UI programming with XAML-technologies. 2008 I wrote my first 1000+-pages book about Microsoft's UI-Framework Windows Presentation Foundation (WPF), followed by some more books about Silverlight and Windows Store Apps.

Beside writing books, I enjoy to write articles, to speak at conferences and to author video trainings for Pluralsight. But of course, beside all these great things I do some "real work". I work in Switzerland for a service-provider called Trivadis as a developer, consultant, trainer and architect.

More and more projects I'm working on are developed with TypeScript and Angular with a backend in the Cloud. And to be honest: I'm totally fascinated by TypeScript! That is the main reason why I decided to write this book.

I wrote this book for you and not for me!

I want to share my fascination about TypeScript with you and I want to show you why TypeScript is such a great language to work with. If you love C# or if you love Java, I'm sure you'll love TypeScript!

When I'm not coding, I love to spent time with my family. I live in Germany's beautiful black forest with my wife Julia and our 3 daughters Anna, Sara and Elsa. I like playing football (=soccer), and for some years I was a captain of a football-team. I also like playing guitar, working out, snowboarding and riding into the sunset with my motorcycle.

Find more information about me on my personal website on www.thomasclaudiushuber.com

So far so good. Now let's set up your environment so that you can start coding with TypeScript!

2. Setting up Your Environment

Introduction

You learn in this chapter how to set up your environment, so that you can start programming with TypeScript. You learn how to install Node.js and Node Package Manager, how to install TypeScript and how to install Visual Studio Code.

Install Node.js and NPM

Node.js is a JavaScript runtime built on top of Google Chrome's V8 JavaScript engine. Node.js can be used on the server-side to run JavaScript. Node.js comes bundled with the Node Package Manager, or short npm. Npm is used to install node packages – typically JavaScript-libraries - like for example TypeScript or Angular.

To install Node.js with npm, go to www.nodejs.org. There you find two downloads like shown in figure 2.1:
- a long-term support (LTS) version
- a current version with the latest features

Figure 2.1: Download Node.js and npm from www.nodejs.org

For this book, I used the LTS version, so I would recommend the same to you. After you've downloaded the LTS version, the installation is pretty simple. Accept the license and click a few times on the next-button and you're done!

Congrats, now you have Node.js and npm on your machine. Now you're ready to install TypeScript.

Install TypeScript

In the previous section, you've installed npm that comes bundled with Node.js. Now you can use npm to install TypeScript. Just fire up a command line window and enter this command:

```
npm install -g typescript
```

The command above tells npm to install the typescript package on your machine. With the -g-parameter npm installs the package globally on your machine, and not just locally in the current folder you're in.

When a package is installed globally, its commands are registered on your system, so that you can use them from the command line. In case of the typescript package you've now the TypeScript compiler (tsc) installed and added to your path environment variable. You can check the installed TypeScript compiler version on the command line with this command:

```
tsc -v
```

Great. Now you've installed TypeScript on your machine. Let's add a code editor and ensure you have a great browser to work with. Then you're ready to write some TypeScript code.

> **Note**
>
> You can search npm packages on www.npmjs.com. You find the TypeScript-package here: https://www.npmjs.com/package/typescript
>
> You also find documentation on that website about how to use the npm command line interface to create your own packages.
>
> In chapter 9, "Modules", you learn more about npm and the *package.json*-file when setting up SystemJS as a module loader.

Install Visual Studio Code

There are several great code editors for TypeScript and JavaScript out there like WebStorm or Sublime. Personally, I'm a huge fan of Visual Studio Code. It's fast, it's lightweight and it's free. In this book, I use Visual Studio Code, but you can use any other editor if you want.

To install Visual Studio Code, go to http://code.visualstudio.com. There you find downloads for Windows, Mac OS and Linux. Download the version for your operating system and install it. The installation wizard on windows contains a page that allows you to add an "Open with code" menu item to Windows Explorer's context menu. I recommend you to check this option for the file as well as for the directory context menu. Figure 2.2 shows you what I selected on my machine. The "Open with code"-option is very comfortable to open Visual Studio Code directly out of any folder on your system via Windows Explorer's context menu.

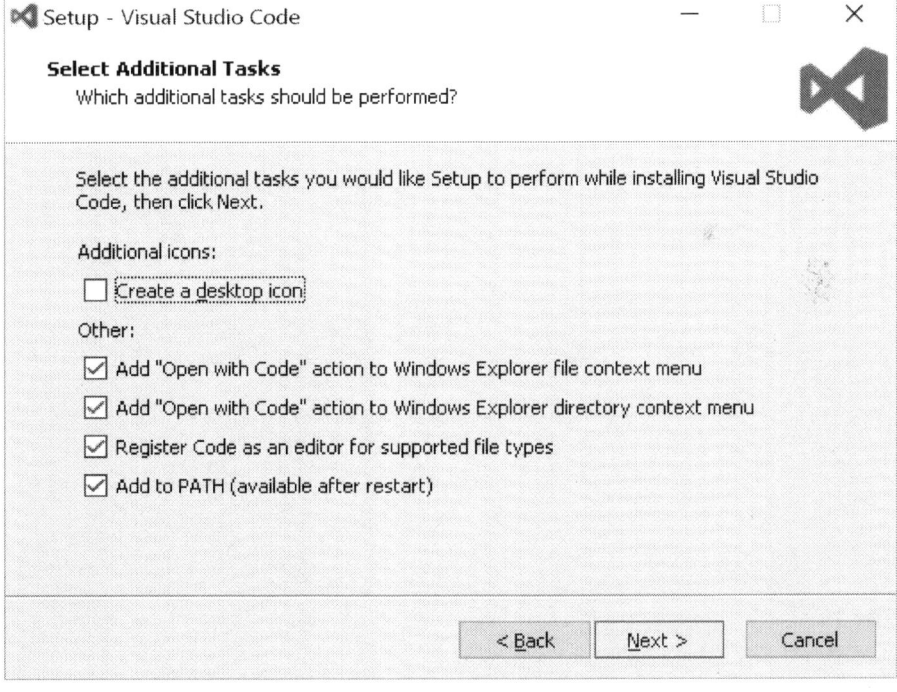

Figure 2.2: Adding "Open with Code" to Windows Explorer

Install Google Chrome

You can use any browser you like to run your JavaScript code. In this book, I'm using Google Chrome, as I think not only the browser itself, but also its developer tools are fantastic. You can open up the developer tools in Google Chrome and in most other browsers by pressing F12. You can download Google Chrome from https://chrome.google.com.

Summary

Congrats! You've installed
- Node.js with npm
- TypeScript
- Visual Studio Code
- Google Chrome

Now you're ready to write some code.

3. Using TypeScript

Introduction

In this chapter, you'll take a plain JavaScript-file that you migrate to a TypeScript-file. You learn how to compile the TypeScript-file and how to get compile-time errors by adding types to your code. You'll also learn how to parameterize the TypeScript compiler, so that you can compile to different JavaScript versions like ES5 or ES2015.

> **Note**
>
> You find the official TypeScript documentation on www.typescriptlang.org

Run a Simple, Buggy JavaScript File

Listing 3.1 shows the content of a simple JavaScript-file called *main.js*. A `printFirstNames`-function takes a `friends`-parameter. The function loops over the friends with a for-loop. For each friend, it logs the content of the `firstName`-property to the browser's console.

```
function printFirstNames(friends) {
    for (let friend of friends) {
        console.log(friend.firstName);
    }
}
printFirstNames(7);
```

Listing 3.1: *03\starter\main.js*

After the function is declared, it is called. A number 7 is passed in to the function. Of course, the `printFirstNames`-function expects an array as input, and not just a simple number. But in JavaScript you don't get a compile-time error here, instead you will get a runtime error when the code is executed. But hey, how do you actually run that *main.js*-file?

Open up Visual Studio Code for that folder containing the *main.js*-file. Add a new html-file to the folder called *index.html*. The *index.html*-file needs to have the content shown in listing 3.2.

```
<!DOCTYPE html>
<html>
  <head>
    <title>Getting started with TypeScript</title>
  </head>
  <body>
    <script src="main.js"></script>
  </body>
</html>
```

Listing 3.2: 03\done\index.html

As you can see, the body of the *index.html*-file in listing 3.2 contains a `script`-element. The `src`-attribute of the `script`-element points to the *main.js*-file to load it. When a `script`-element is placed in the body of an html-page, the referenced script is executed when the body is parsed at startup. In your case this is exactly what you want: You want to execute the JavaScript code from the *main.js*-file when the html-page is loaded by the browser.

> **Note**
>
> When you don't want to execute JavaScript code at startup, you have to place the `script`-element inside of the `head`-element of the html-page, and not inside of the `body`-element. Then the JavaScript code is loaded by the browser, but not executed. Then you can call your functions manually, for example when a button is clicked.

Now let's open the *index.html*-file in the browser. To do this, you can either just double-click the file in Windows Explorer – if you're running Windows - or you can open up an integrated terminal in Visual Studio Code via main menu "View→Integrated Terminal" (figure 3.1). In that terminal, type in this statement:

```
start index.html
```

This will open up the *index.html*-file as if you would have clicked it in Windows Explorer. But using this approach with the integrated terminal, you don't have to leave your code editor to startup the *index.html*-file. Most developers love it to stay in their code editor.

Chapter 3, "Using TypeScript"

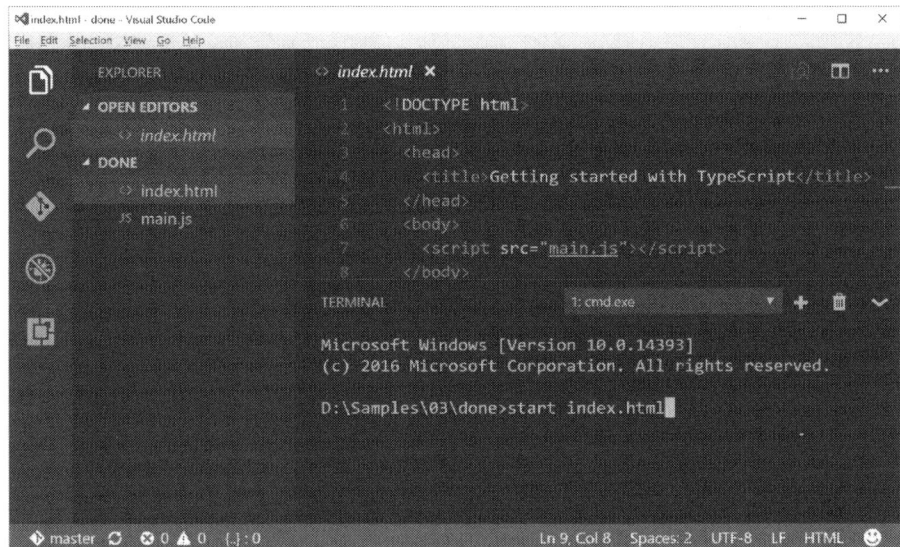

Figure 3.1: Start the index.html from Visual Studio Code's Integrated Terminal

Now you've Google Chrome running the *index.html*-file. Open up the developer tools by pressing F12. Switch to the Console tab like in figure 3.2. Note that the Console has logged an error.

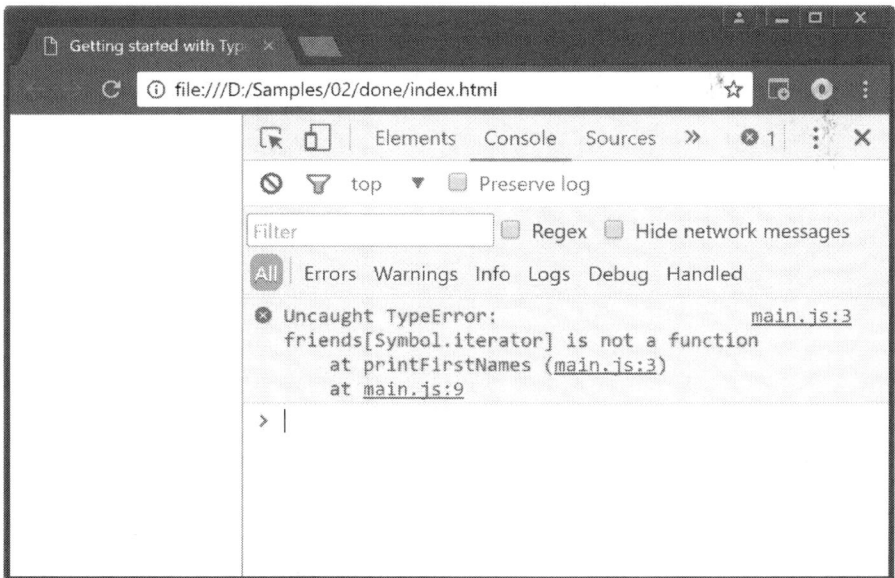

Figure 3.2: The console logs a TypeError.

27

The for-loop in the JavaScript code (Listing 3.1) tries to iterate over the number 7. But the number 7 is no array, so it can't be iterated and you get the error shown in figure 3.2. Don't fix this error. At least not yet. Instead, let's use TypeScript to get a compile-time error.

Introduce TypeScript

To use TypeScript, just rename the *main.js*-file to *main.ts*. When you compile the *main.ts*-file, the output will be a *main.js*-file like it is already referenced in the *index.html*-file. To kick off the TypeScript compiler that will generate the *main.js*-file, just type this command into Visual Studio Code's integrated terminal:

```
tsc main.ts
```

This command will compile the *main.ts*-file once. After you've changed the TypeScript code, you have to run the command again to get the compiled JavaScript in a *main.js*-file. But I'm sure you are like all developers: You don't want to run that statement after every change in your *main.ts*-file. And the great thing is: You don't have to. You can start the TypeScript compiler in watch mode by specifying the -w parameter:

```
tsc main.ts -w
```

Now the TypeScript compiler will generate the *main.js*-file, whenever the *main.ts*-file is changed and saved. You can stop the watch-mode by pressing CTRL+C in the terminal.

Ok, so far so good. You're compiling the TypeScript code to JavaScript, and you've turned on watch mode by specifying the -w parameter.

Note that you didn't adjust the JavaScript code itself. As TypeScript is a superset of JavaScript, it just works. All you did was renaming the file from *main.js* to *main.ts*. With the TypeScript compiler, the *main.ts*-file is compiled to JavaScript that is written to the compiler-generated *main.js*-file. That means at runtime, the browser is using classic JavaScript. TypeScript is just part of your development process.

> **Note**
>
> It's also possible to let the browser compile the TypeScript code to JavaScript on the fly. That's ok during development and prototyping if you need it. But when you deploy your app, you want it to be as fast as possible. That means you pre-compile your TypeScript code to JavaScript before you deploy. And pre-compiling TypeScript is also the most common approach during development. So, this pre-compiling approach is also used throughout this book.

Add and Use an Interface

So far you don't get any errors in your *main.ts*-file. That's because there are no types involved. Listing 3.3 adds a `Friend`-interface that has a `firstName`-property of type string. This `Friend`-interface is used to define the type of the parameter of the `printFirstNames`-function. In listing 3.3, the parameter is now an array of `Friend`-objects (`Friend[]`):

```typescript
interface Friend {
    firstName: string;
}
function printFirstNames(friends: Friend[]) {
    for (let friend of friends) {
        console.log(friend.firstName);
    }
}
printFirstNames(7);
```

Listing 3.3: Adding an interface to the main.ts-file

With the interface in place, the TypeScript compiler logs an error for the line where the `printFirstNames`-function is called with the number 7. You can see the error in the integrated terminal from which you've started the TypeScript compiler in watch mode:

```
main.ts(9,17): error TS2345: Argument of type '7' is not assignable to parameter of type 'Friend[]'.
```

Even Visual Studio Code adds a red squiggle under the number 7 that is passed to the `printFirstNames`-function. The tooltip shows the error (figure 3.3).

```
    4    function printFirstNames(friends: Friend[]) {
    5        for (let friend of friends) {
    6            console log(friend firstName);
```
[ts] Argument of type '7' is not assignable to parameter of typ
e 'Friend[]'.
```
    9    printFirstNames(7);
   10
```

Figure 3.3: Visual Studio Code shows the error in a tooltip

> **Note**
>
> You might find out that the TypeScript compiler still emits the JavaScript code, even if there is an error like the one from figure 3.3. When you don't want the compiler to emit the JavaScript code when there are errors, you can set the `noEmitOnError` compiler option. You set this option usually in a config-file for the compiler that is called *tsconfig.json*. You learn how to generate and use such a *tsconfig.json*-file later in this chapter.

Fix the Code

With the defined `Friend`-interface, you can fix the code easily. Instead of passing a simple number to the `printFirstNames`-function, you pass in an array of objects that have a `firstName`-property. As Visual Studio Code knows about the required type, it gives you even statement completion for the `firstName`-property (figure 3.4).

```
    9    printFirstNames([
   10       {f}
   11        ● firstName         (property) Friend.firstName: string
            □ for
            □ foreach =>
            □ forin
            □ function
```

Figure 3.4: Visual Studio Code gives you statement completion

Listing 3.4 shows the fixed code.

An array with three objects is passed to the `printFirstNames`-function. Every object has a `firstName`-property like required by the `Friend`-interface

```
printFirstNames([
    { firstName: "Thomas" },
    { firstName: "Julia" },
    { firstName: "Anna" }
]);
```
Listing 3.4: 03\done\main.ts

If you didn't start the TypeScript compiler in watch mode, compile the *main.ts*-file with the fixed code by calling `tsc main.ts` on the command line. When you refresh the *index.html*-page in Google Chrome, you can see that the firstnames of the three objects are written to the browser's console (figure 3.5).

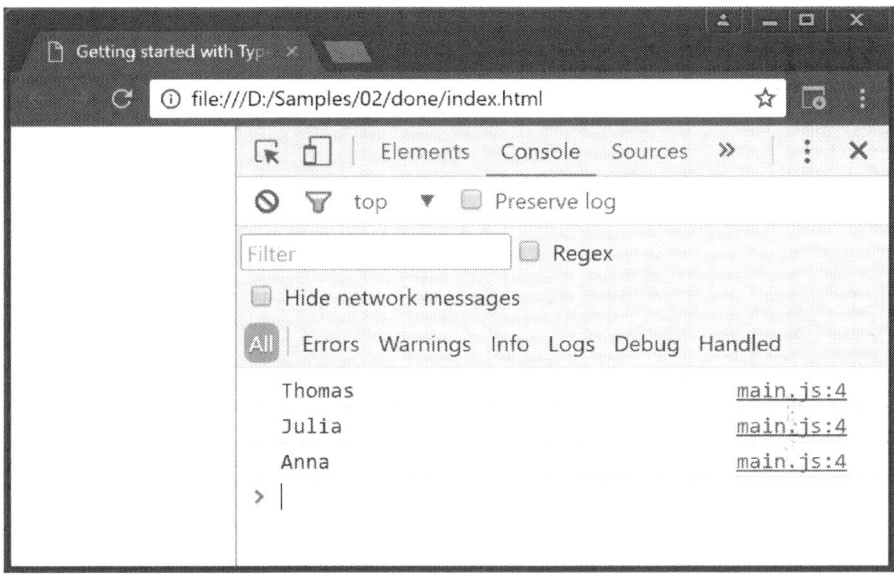

Figure 3.5: The firstnames are written to the browser's console

Define Compiler Options

You fixed the code, but you didn't look at the compiled JavaScript code so far, or did you? If not, open the generated *main.js*-file, and you'll see the content shown in listing 3.5.

```
function printFirstNames(friends) {
    for (var _i = 0, friends_1 = friends; _i < friends_1.length;
        _i++) {
        var friend = friends_1[_i];
        console.log(friend.firstName);
    }
}
printFirstNames([
    { firstName: "Thomas" },
    { firstName: "Julia" },
    { firstName: "Anna" }
]);
```

Listing 3.5: *03\done\main.js*

There are some things to note when looking at the compiled JavaScript code of listing 3.5: The Friend-interface does not appear in JavaScript. An interface is only available in TypeScript, but not in JavaScript. This means an interface is only part of your development process.

The second thing to note about listing 3.5 is that the generated code is classic JavaScript, there are no types anymore, and nothing TypeScript specific. This code runs in any browser that supports that JavaScript version. But hey, what is actually the JavaScript version that you got out of your TypeScript code? And what the heck happened to the for-of-loop in listing 3.5?

By default, the TypeScript compiler compiles your code to ES3. The for-of-loop that you have used in TypeScript is available in JavaScript since ES2015. That means the default version used by the compiler (ES3) does not support the for-of-loop. Of course, the TypeScript compiler knows this, and so it generates a classic for-loop like in listing 3.5.

But you can define the target JavaScript version with the compiler parameter -t. Some possible values for it are es3, es5, es2015, es2016, es2017. If you want to compile to es2015, where the for-of-loop is supported, you can use this command:

```
tsc main.ts -t "es2015"
```

Run this command and look at the generated *main.js*-file. It has now the for-of-loop, as it is supported with ES2015. Listing 3.6 shows that ES2015-code.

```
function printFirstNames(friends) {
    for (let friend of friends) {
        console.log(friend.firstName);
    }
}
printFirstNames([
    { firstName: "Thomas" },
    { firstName: "Julia" },
    { firstName: "Anna" }
]);
```

Listing 3.6: *The generated main.js-file has a for-of-loop for ES2015 or later*

The ES2015-code of listing 3.6 looks like the TypeScript code we've written, just without the types.

Create and Use a tsconfig.json-file

The TypeScript compiler supports several options to specify how the JavaScript code is generated. You learned in the previous section about the -t parameter to define the target JavaScript version. There are a bunch more parameters that the compiler supports.

> **Note**
> A complete overview of the available compiler options is available in the official TypeScript handbook on https://www.typescriptlang.org/docs/handbook/compiler-options.html

Passing the parameters on a command line is fine if you try out stuff on your own. But if you work on a team or if you share your code, you might want that every developer compiles the TypeScript code with the same options as you did. To ensure this, you need to define the compiler options in some config-file. And such a config-file is supported out-of-the-box by the TypeScript compiler:

It's called *tsconfig.json*.

Before you jump over to your keyboard to create such a file, wait! Just go to the command line and enter this command, then the TypeScript compiler creates a *tsconfig.json*-file for you:

```
tsc --init
```

The generated *tsconfig.json*-file looks like shown in listing 3.7.

```
{
    "compilerOptions": {
        "module": "commonjs",
        "target": "es5",
        "noImplicitAny": false,
        "sourceMap": false
    }
}
```

Listing 3.7: 02\done\tsconfig.json

You know already about the `target`-option. It allows you to specify values like es3, es5, es2015, es2016 etc. Note that the generated *tsconfig.json*-file contains the target version es5.

The `module`-option in listing 3.7 is important when you are using modules in TypeScript. You learn more about modules in chapter 9, "Modules".

The `noImplicitAny`-option can be set to `true` if you want the compiler to raise an error if a type is not specified and the compiler implicitly assumes the `any` type. You learn more about the `any` type in chapter 4, "Basic Types".

The `sourceMap`-option can be set to `true` if you want the compiler to generate *.js.map*-files. These files make it possible that you step through your TypeScript code when debugging, and not through the generated JavaScript code. More to debugging in the next section of this chapter.

Now you have your *tsconfig.json*-file in place. To start the compiler, just go to the command line or Visual Studio Code's integrated terminal and enter this simple and brilliant command:

```
tsc
```

The TypeScript compiler will look for the *tsconfig.json*-file and will use the options from that file. If you want to start the compiler in watch mode, run the `tsc`-command with the `-w` parameter on the command line:

```
tsc -w
```

That's it! Now you have your compiler options in a nice *tsconfig.json*-file. For the rest of this book, a *tsconfig.json*-file is used for all samples. That means to compile the TypeScript code, you just call `tsc` on the command line.

> **Note**
>
> Don't specify the filename if you want to use the *tsconfig.json*-file with the compiler. When you call the compiler for example with `tsc main.ts -w`, the compiler won't read the *tsconfig.json*-file. So just use `tsc` or `tsc -w`.

Debug your TypeScript Code

When you run your *index.html*-file in Google Chrome, you can debug your code. Open the developer tools by pressing F12. In the developer tools, switch to the Sources-Tab. There you can select the *main.js*-file and set a breakpoint in the code - like in figure 3.6 on the `console.log`-function.

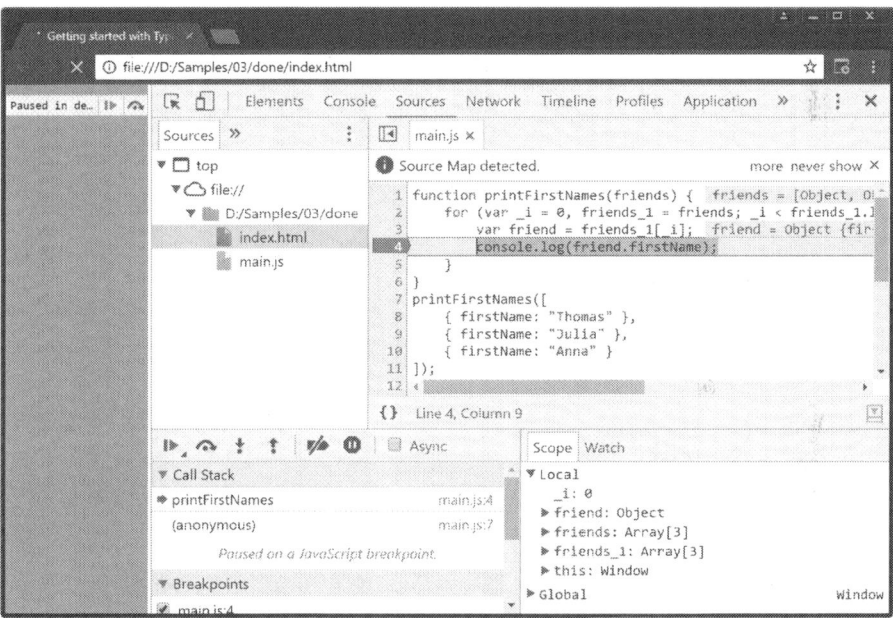

Figure 3.6: Adding a breakpoint in the JavaScript code

With the breakpoint set, you can refresh the page to execute the JavaScript code. Then the breakpoint will be hit like in figure 3.6. You can continue with F8, step over a function with F10 and step into a function with F11. Instead of using these keys you can also use the nice buttons in the Chrome developer tools.

But wait a minute: Do you really have to debug the compiled JavaScript code? You have written TypeScript. It would be much better to set breakpoints in your TypeScript code instead of setting breakpoints in the generated JavaScript code. Especially if your code is more complex than in this sample you might find it a pain if you're not able to set breakpoints in your TypeScript code.

To be able to set breakpoints in your TypeScript code, the browser needs a *.map*-file. Such a *.map*-file maps lines and tokens of the compiled JavaScript code to your TypeScript code. This allows the browser to hit breakpoints in your TypeScript code.

To generate a *.map*-file for each compiler generated *.js*-file, you need to set the `sourceMap`-compiler option in your *tsconfig.json*-file to true:

```
{
    "compilerOptions": {
        "module": "commonjs",
        "target": "es5",
        "noImplicitAny": false,
        "sourceMap": true
    }
}
```

Listing 3.8: *02\done\tsconfig.json*

In case of the *main.ts*-file, the TypeScript compiler will now generate not only a *main.js*-file, but also a *main.js.map*-file that contains the mappings from JavaScript to TypeScript. And just the existence of that *main.js.map*-file is enough that you can set breakpoints in your TypeScript code.

After you've compiled your code again to generate the *.map*-file, start the *index.html*-file again in Google Chrome. Switch to the Sources-Tab of the developer tools. Now you see the *main.ts*-file that gets loaded by the browser, because the browser reads the *main.js.map*-file that has a pointer to the *main.ts*-file. Now you can set breakpoints in your TypeScript code like in figure 3.7. Happy TypeScript debugging!

Chapter 3, "Using TypeScript"

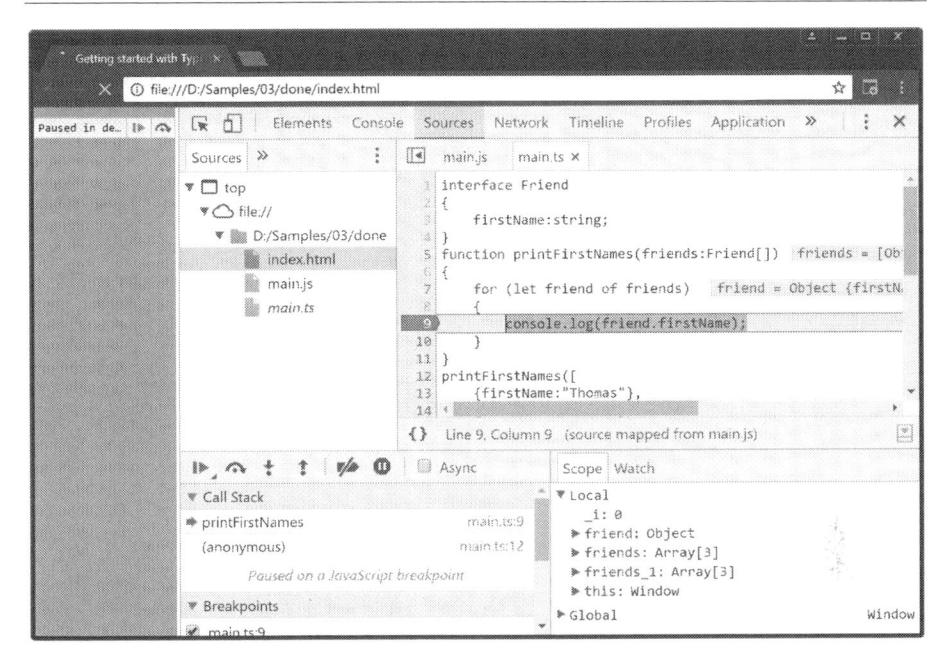

figure 3.7: Setting breakpoints in your TypeScript code

With the included *.map*-file, the directory with the code has now these five files:

- *index.html*
- *main.js*
- *main.js.map*
- *main.ts*
- *tsconfig.json*

Hide JS in Visual Studio Code

The compiled *.js*-files and *.js.map*-files can add a lot of visual noise in Visual Studio Code. This gets even more when you have multiple *.ts*-files and so multiple generated *.js*-files and *.js.map*-files. Luckily, Visual Studio Code is a very flexible editor. It allows you to hide these files if you want.

Go to the main menu and select File • Preferences • User Settings. This opens up a *settings.json*-file in a split-view like in figure 3.8. On the left side, you find the default settings, and on the right side you can overwrite these default settings with your own settings.

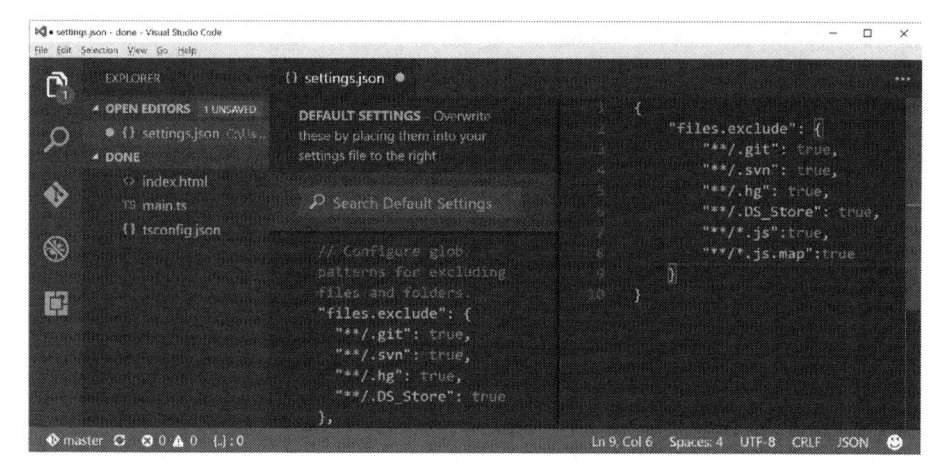

Figure 3.8: Settings to hide .js-files and .js.map-files

In figure 3.8 you can see that the setting `files.exclude` is overwritten. It contains in addition to the default setting the files *.js* and *.js.map*, so that these files are excluded in the Explorer of Visual Studio Code. Now look at the Explorer in figure 3.8, the files `main.js` and `main.js.map` are hidden.

But wait, maybe you want to hide a *.js*-file only if there's a corresponding *.ts*-file. You can even do that with this setting:

```
{
    "files.exclude": {
        "**/.git": true,
        "**/.svn": true,
        "**/.hg": true,
        "**/.DS_Store": true,
        "**/*.js":{"when": "$(basename).ts"},
        "**/*.js.map":true
    }
}
```

Note
In bigger projects, you might want to generate your JavaScript code in a complete different directory than the one that contains your TypeScript code. To do this, you can use a task runner like for example Gulp (http://www.gulpjs.com). With Gulp, you can copy files around and you can compile TypeScript with the gulp-typescript module that is also available as a Node Package via npm.

Summary

In this chapter, you learned how to migrate from JavaScript to TypeScript by renaming the file-extension from *.js* to *.ts*. You learned how to compile TypeScript code and how to use an interface to get compile-time errors.

You've also learned how to compile to different ECMAScript versions by using the target-compiler option. You also know how to specify compiler options in a *tsconfig.json*-file that can be generated with `tsc -init`.

By calling `tsc -w`, you start the TypeScript compiler in watch mode, then it compiles the *.ts*-files whenever you've made changes to them.

If you want to set breakpoints in your TypeScript code for a debugging session, you have to create *.map*-files by setting the `sourceMap`-compiler option to `true`.

So far you know about the fundamentals of TypeScript. Now it's time to learn about the basic types supported by TypeScript, like number, string and boolean.

4. Basic Types

Introduction

This chapter shows you the basic types available in TypeScript, like string, number and boolean. In addition, you learn about arrays, tuples, enums, the any-type, union types and how to handle undefined and null in TypeScript by turning on the "strict null checking" compiler option.

Beside all that, you learn about TypeScript's type inference feature that automatically infers a variable's type based on the assignment. You also learn about type assertions, which is from the syntactical point of view similar to a casting in classic languages like C# or Java.

Ok, are you ready? Let's begin with the simplest type available in TypeScript, the boolean-type.

Boolean

The boolean-type lets you specify either the value `true` or `false` for a variable:

```
let isVisible: boolean = true;
```

As you can see in the code line above, the type is annotated after the variable-name. A colon separates the variable-name and the type. This is the syntax used by TypeScript, and you use this syntax also to annotate variables with other types like string, number etc.

> **Note**
> The `let`-keyword is used to define a variable. If you are familiar with classic JavaScript, you might know the `var`-keyword. You learn more about `var` and `let` in chapter 5, "Var, Let and Const".

When you have defined a variable of a specific type like boolean, you can't assign objects of different types to that variable anymore. For example, when you try to assign a string to a boolean-variable, you get a compile-time error:

```
let isVisible: boolean = true;
isVisible = "hidden"; // Error: string not assignable to boolean
```

Type Inference

When you assign a value to a variable at its declaration, TypeScript can infer the variable's type. That means you can omit the type annotation. Look at the `isVisible`-variable in listing 4.1. It is implicitly of type boolean, as TypeScript infers that type from the assigned value `true`:

```
let isVisible = true; // TypeScript infers the type boolean
isVisible = "hidden"; // Error: string not assignable to boolean
```

Listing 4.1: Type inference in TypeScript

But be aware: When you split the declaration and the assignment of your variable, TypeScript cannot infer the type and falls back to the any type that you see later in this chapter:

```
let isVisible; // declaration without type annotation
isVisible = true; // assignment of bool
isVisible = "hidden"; // WORKS!!! No compile-time error
```

Listing 4.2: 04\01_boolean\main.ts

So, whenever you split the declaration and the assignment, you have to explicitly set the type annotation to get compile-time errors if another type is assigned:

```
let isVisible: boolean; // declaration with type annotation
isVisible = true; // assignment of bool
isVisible = "hidden"; // Error: string not assignable to boolean
```

Listing 4.3: 04\01_boolean\main.ts

The type inference described in this section works not only for the boolean-type, but also for other types. If the TypeScript compiler can infer the type at compile-time, it uses that type.

> **Note**
>
> In this book, you find many code listings where types are annotated explicitly, even when the TypeScript compiler can infer the types. Like for example in this statement:
>
> ```
> let isVisible: boolean = true;
> ```
>
> The `boolean`-annotation could be omitted, and the TypeScript compiler infers the type based on the assignment. But being explicit with a type annotation makes the code especially for beginners clear and simple to understand. You don't have to think what type it is.
>
> But later when we work with classes, we omit the type annotation mostly, as it is obvious what object it is when you call a constructor with `new`.
>
> So instead of
>
> ```
> let dev: Developer = new Developer("Thomas");
> ```
>
> we use this
>
> ```
> let dev = new Developer("Thomas");
> ```

Number

Numbers in TypeScript are of type `number`:

```
let width: number = 2;
```

As you know, TypeScript is a superset of JavaScript. And unlike to languages like C# or Java, JavaScript does not define different types for numbers like integer, short, long or float. In JavaScript, and so in TypeScript, all numbers are 64-bit floating point numbers. That means you can also assign a number with decimals to your variable:

```
let width: number = 2.54;
```

TypeScript also supports number-literals in the form of hex, binary and octal. These four number-variables contain all the same value, 27:

```
let dec: number = 27;
let hex: number = 0x001b;
let binary: number = 0b11011;
let octal: number= 0o0033;
```

Listing 4.4: 04\02_number\main.ts

String

To create a string-variable, you use the string-type in TypeScript. You can put the assigned string in double-quotes or in single-quotes.

```
let firstName: string = "Thomas";
firstName = 'Tom'; // like in JavaScript single-quotes work as well
```

TypeScript also supports template strings by using back-ticks instead of quotes. You can include expressions in such a template string by using the syntax ${ expression } in your string:

```
let firstName: string ="Thomas";
let message: string = `Welcome ${firstName}, how are you?`;
```

You can even add line breaks in a template string:

```
let message: string = `Welcome ${firstName},
how are you?`;
```

Listing 4.5: 04\03_string\main.ts

When you look at the generated JavaScript from the TypeScript code of listing 4.5, you can see this classic string concatenation if you compiled to ES5 or ES3:

```
var message = "Welcome " + firstName + ",\nhow are you?";
```

Listing 4.6: 04\03_string\main.js

Note the line break with \n in the generated JavaScript code of listing 4.6. When you compile to ES2015 or later, the template strings are supported natively in JavaScript. You can try this by changing the target compiler option in your *tsconfig.json*-file to es2015. Then the compiled JavaScript code contains exactly the same template string as the TypeScript code:

```
let message = `Welcome ${firstName},
how are you?`;
```

Listing 4.7: Generated ES2015 code

To give you more insights about how such a template string and some TypeScript code can play together with HTML, you find a little project in the folder *04\04_stringPlayingWithHtmlElements* of the book samples.

The *index.html*-file of that project has an input field. When you type into that field, you see a message that shows the value of the input field and the length of the value like in figure 4.1.

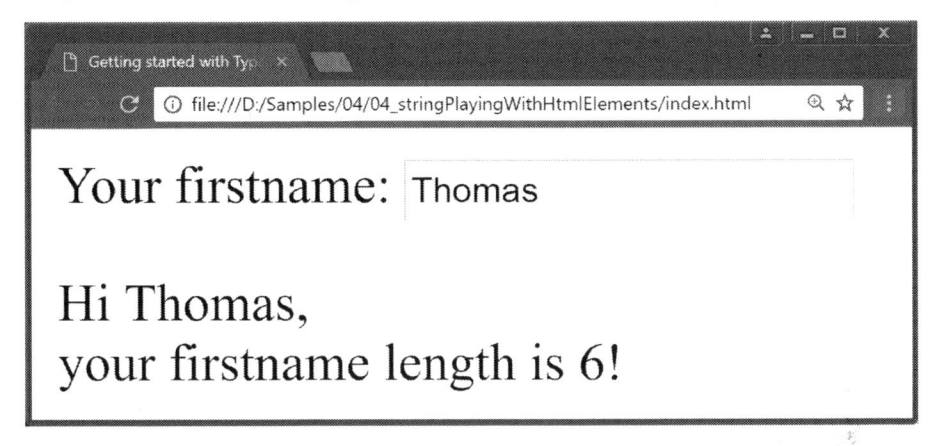

Figure 4.1: The entered firstname and its length are displayed

Listing 4.8 shows the *index.html*-file of this little project. The *main.js*-file is loaded in the head of the page, so that it does not execute on startup. The body contains a `label` and an `input` element. Note that the `onkeyup`-event of the `input` element points to an `onKeyUp`-function. Also, note that the `id`-attributes are set on the `input` and on the `span` element. They are used in TypeScript to grab these two elements.

```html
<!DOCTYPE html>
<html>
  <head>
    <title>Getting started with TypeScript</title>
    <script src="main.js"></script>
  </head>
  <body>
    <div>
      <label>Your firstname:</label>
      <input type="text" id="myInput" onkeyup="onKeyUp()"/>
    </div>
    <p><span id="myOutput"></span></p>
  </body>
</html>
```

Listing 4.8: *04\04_stringPlayingWithHtmlElements\index.html*

When you type, the `onKeyUp`-function is executed. That function is defined in the *main.ts*-file in listing 4.9. The function grabs the `input` element and reads its value. Then it grabs the `span` element and uses a template string to create and assign a message to the `innerText`-property of the `span` element.

```
function onKeyUp() {
  // Grab the input element and its value
  let input = document.getElementById("myInput") as HTMLInputElement;
  let firstname= input.value;

  // Grab the output element
  let output = document.getElementById("myOutput");

  // assign the message to the span-element's innerText-property
  output.innerText = `Hi ${firstname},
your firstname length is ${firstname.trim().length}!`;
}
```
Listing 4.9: 04\04_stringPlayingWithHtmlElements\main.ts

> **Note**
>
> You might have noticed the `as` operator on the first line of listing 4.9:
>
> `let input = document.getElementById("myInput") as HTMLInputElement;`
>
> That's a type assertion. It tells the TypeScript compiler that the returned object of the `getElmentById`-function is an `HTMLInputElement`. Then the TypeScript compiler knows that the object stored in the `input`-variable has a `value`-property that you can access with statement completion:
>
> `let firstname= input.value;`
>
> You read more about type assertions later in this chapter.

Arrays

In TypeScript, you can work – like in JavaScript - with an array of values. You create an array-variable by adding a square bracket pair to the variable-type. This statement declares a `firstNames`-variable that has the type of a string array. The assigned array contains three strings:

```
let firstNames: string[] = ["Thomas", "Sara", "Julia"];
```

TypeScript gives you another option to define the type of an array-variable: The generic `Array` class. The following code line does the same as the previous code line– it creates and initializes a string array with three strings:

```
let firstNames: Array<string> = ["Thomas", "Sara", "Julia"];
```

If you use square brackets or the generic `Array`-class is just a matter of personal preference.

Iterating Arrays: for...of and for...in

To iterate the values of an array, you use a for-of-loop. This loop will log Julia, Anna and Thomas to the browser's console:

```
let firstnames: string[] = ["Julia", "Anna", "Thomas"];
for (let firstname of firstnames) {
   console.log(firstname);
}
```

Listing 4.10: 04\05_array\main.ts

There's also a for-in-loop available in TypeScript. It looks similar to the for-of-loop, the only difference is the keyword `in` instead of `of`. Such a for-in-loop on an array does not return the values themselves, but the indexes of all the values:

```
let firstnames: string[] = ["Julia", "Anna", "Thomas"];
for (let index in firstnames) {
   console.log(`${index} - ${firstnames[index]}`);
}
```

Listing 4.11: 04\05_array\main.ts

The code of listing 4.11 prints these values to the brower's console:

```
0 - Julia
1 - Anna
2 - Thomas
```

For... in on Objects

The for-in-loop can not only be used on arrays, but also on classic objects to iterate an object's properties. When you use it on an object, it gives you back the member names. Let's assume you have created a friend like this:

```
interface Friend {
    firstName:string;
    lastName:string;
}
let friend: Friend ={firstName:"Thomas",lastName:"Huber"};
```

Listing 4.12: 04\06_forInOnObject\main.ts

As TypeScript is JavaScript, you can access the friend's `firstName`-property in two ways, either with the dot-operator or with square brackets:

```
let firstName = friend.firstName; // Using the dot operator
firstName = friend["firstName"]; // Using square brackets
```

The square brackets are great to use with a for-in-loop, as you get the member names in such a for-in-loop. You can do for example something like in listing 4.13 to print out the property names and their values:

```
for (let propName in friend) {
    console.log(`${propName}: ${friend[propName]}`);
}
```

Listing 4.13: 04\06_forInOnObject\main.ts

The for-in-loop of listing 4.13 will print this to the browser's console:

```
firstName: Thomas
lastName: Huber
```

Tuples

Tuples are like arrays, but they can have different types. The code line below contains a tuple with a `string` and a `boolean`:

```
let nameIsDev: [string, boolean] = ["Thomas", true];
```

The `string` is at index 0, and the `boolean` is at index 1. TypeScript knows this and does a type checking when you assign new values:

```
nameIsDev[1] = false; // OK
nameIsDev[1] = "yes"; // Error: Not assignable to boolean
```

Unlike in other languages, tuples in TypeScript are not fixed to their length. So, you can assign a value to a larger index that does not exist on your tuple. But what will be the type of that value? It can be any type the tuple is already using:

```
let nameIsDev: [string, boolean] = ["Thomas", true];
nameIsDev[2] = "yes"; // Works, as tuple has string
nameIsDev[2] = false; // Works, as tuple has boolean
nameIsDev[2] = 1; // Error: 1 is not assignable to string|boolean
```

Behind the scenes, TypeScript uses a union type if you extend the tuple. In the snippet above the used union type is `string | boolean`. You read more about union types later in this chapter.

Enums

With enums you can give friendly names to a set of numbers. By default, the enum starts with the number 0 for the first name, and then just counts up that number for the next names. So, this `Dock` enum has the number 0 for `left`, 1 for `top`, 2 for `right` and 3 for `bottom`:

```
enum Dock { left, top, right, bottom }
```

You can also set another start number:

```
enum Dock { left = 1, top, right, bottom }
```

Or you can set all numbers explicitly:

```
enum Dock { left = 0, top = 1, right = 2, bottom = 3 }
```

To access a value of the enum, you use the enum name followed by the member name:

```
let dock: Dock = Dock.top;
```

As the enum is just a set of friendly names for numbers, you can also assign the value of an enum directly to a number-variable:

```
let val: number = Dock.top;
```

When you use enums, you often find yourself wanting to go from the number to the name. You can do it like this:

```
let valName: string = Dock[1]; // valName will be "top"
```

You can also use a concrete enum-value to get the friendly name:

```
let valName: string = Dock[Dock.top]; // valName will be "top"
```

Beside getting the name for a number or an enum value, you might find a need for the opposite scenario where you have a string and you want to have the enum value or the number. Getting these from a string "top" is as simple like this:

```
let num: number = Dock["top"];
let dock: Dock = Dock["top"];
```

> **Note**
>
> Enums are a TypeScript concept. They don't exist in JavaScript. Behind the scenes arrays and numbers are used. If you're curious, just take a look at the generated JavaScript code.

The any type

Sometimes you need the dynamic behaviour of JavaScript, and not the static typing of TypeScript. Then you can use the any-type in TypeScript.

```
let isVisible: any = true;  // Initialized with boolean
console.log(typeof isVisible);  // Logs "boolean"

isVisible = "hidden";  // String assignment works as well
console.log(typeof isVisible);  // Logs "string"

isVisible.SomeNonExistingFunction ();
                // No compile-time error, as existence of
                // function is not checked by TypeScript
                // at compile-time
```

The any type tells the TypeScript compiler not to do any checking of the type and of the existence of its members. That is great when you need dynamic code that cannot be evaluated at compile-time. For all other cases where you have the information at compile-time, you should always prefer a concrete type over any, as this will give you the type checking and tooling support like statement completion that makes TypeScript so powerful.

Beside simple variables, the any type is quite important when it comes to function-parameters. Function-parameters are implicitly any if you don't specify a type for the parameters. Look at the function below, the friend-parameter is implicitly any:

```
function printFirstName(friend) {
   console.log(friend.firstName);
}
```

Listing 4.14: The friend-parameter is implicitly any

But being explicit is better in most cases, especially if you're using TypeScript. But when you migrate a larger JavaScript code base to TypeScript, you might still have functions without types on the parameters. To find out about these, you can use the TypeScript compiler option called noImplicitAny. Go and set it to true in your *tsconfig.json* like shown in listing 4.15.

```
{
    "compilerOptions": {
        "module": "commonjs",
        "target": "es2015",
        "noImplicitAny": true,
        "sourceMap": false
    }
}
```

Listing 4.15: tsconfig.json with noImplicitAny set to true

With `noImplicitAny` set to `true`, you get compile-time errors for function parameters that are implicitly any. Visual Studio Code underlines these parameters and displays the errors in a tooltip (figure 4.2).

```
function printFirstName(friend) {
    console.lo [ts] Parameter 'friend' implicitly has an 'any' type.
}
           (parameter) friend: any
```

Figure 4.2: Visual Studio Code displays an error for an implicitly any type

To fix the error, you have to explicitly set the types on your function parameters. The any-type is a valid type. But by specifying it, you explicitly are saying this parameter should be any:

```
function printFirstName(friend: any) {
    console.log(friend.firstName);
}
```

The drawback of the any type is that you don't get for example statement completion for the `firstName`-property of a friend. There's also no check if the property exists or not. In case of that `printFirstName`-function, you should prefer an Interface over the any-type, as you know already that the object must have a `firstName`-property. There is no need in this case to use the dynamic behaviour of JavaScript. So, just add an interface like here:

```
interface Friend {
    firstName: string;
}
function printFirstName(friend: Friend) {
    console.log(friend.firstName);
}
```

Type Assertions

Sometimes you might know better than the TypeScript compiler. Let's assume you have a `firstName`-variable and you know that it contains a string, but note that the type is set to any:

```
let firstName: any = "Thomas";
```

When you want to access a property of the string, like for example the `length`-property, you don't get any statement completion for that property, as the type of the `firstName` variable is any:

```
let len: number = firstName.length;
```

You can even write a typo, like "lenth" instead of "length". The TypeScript compiler does not check this, as you're working on the any type. But you know better, it is a string. And you can tell this to the TypeScript compiler by using a type assertion with the as-operator:

```
let len: number = (firstName as string).length;
```

This gives type checking on the `length`-property and statement completion like shown in figure 4.3.

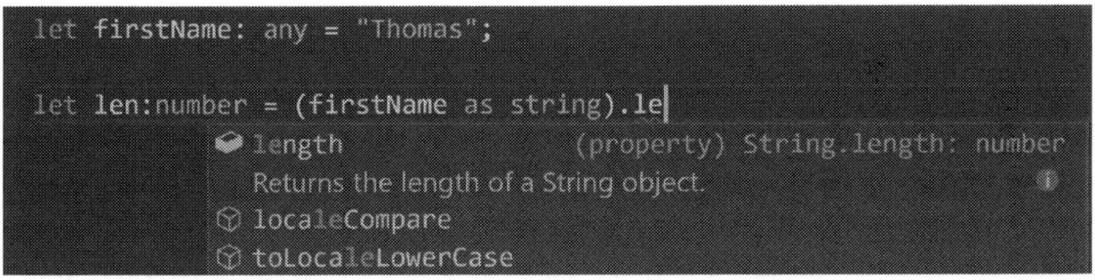

Figure 4.3: You get statement completion with the type assertion

Beside the `as`-operator there's another syntax to write a type assertion using angle brackets:

```
let length: number = (<string>firstName).length;
```

In this book the `as` operator is the preferred syntax for a type assertion.

> **Note**
>
> Originally the type assertion with the angle brackets was the only type assertion syntax available in TypeScript. But if you're using JSX, the angle brackets can lead to problems, as JSX is an XML-like syntax. That's the reason why the as-operator has been introduced as the way to go if you're using JSX. As the as-operator works in all cases, it is the way used in this book.

Type assertions are used quite often when a function returns a base type, and you know already at compile-time about a more specific type. A typical example for this is the getElementById-function. It returns an HTMLElement. But as the TypeScript compiler is not reading your HTML-code, you might know better what kind of HTML element you are grabbing. Let's assume you've defined this input element:

```
<input type="text" id="myInput"/>
```

To access its value-property in your TypeScript code, you might write this:

```
let input = document.getElementById("myInput");
let value: string = input.value;
```

But unfortunately, the value-property does not exist on the returned HTMLElement, so you get an error when accessing the value-property like shown in figure 4.4.

```
let input = document.getElementById("myInput");

let value = input.value;
    [ts] Property 'value' does not exist on type 'HTMLElement'.
```

Figure 4.4: The value property does not exist on the HTMLElement

To fix this error, you have to use a type assertion, as you know that the element will be an HTMLInputElement:

```
let value: string = (input as HTMLInputElement).value;
```

Instead of doing the assertion on the line of code where you access the `value`-property, you can also do it directly where you call the `getElementById`-function:

```
let input = document.getElementById("myInput") as HTMLInputElement;
let value: string = input.value;
```

In the case above, the `input`-variable is implicitly typed. The first line above is equal to this line where the type of the variable is explicitly annotated:

```
let input: HTMLInputElement =
    document.getElementById("myInput") as HTMLInputElement;
```

Union Types

Sometimes you want a variable to be able to store different types. Instead of using any, you can use a union type. A union type is a combination of several types. Just use pipes in a type annotation to define the separate types for your union type.

The following code creates an `isVisible`-variable using the union-type `boolean | number`. You can assign either a `boolean` or a `number` to that variable, but when you try to assign a string, you get an error:

```
let isVisible : boolean|number = true;
isVisible = 1; // OK
isVisible = "yes"; // Error: Not assignable to boolean|number
```

Union types are quite useful at places where you might use the any type. Look at the `append`-function in listing 4.16. It has a `string`-parameter and an `appendix`-parameter of type `any`. If the `appendix`-parameter is a number, it appends that number of spaces to the string and returns the result. If the appendix is a string, it just appends the string and returns the result. If appendix is neither number nor string, the function throws an error.

```
function append(text: string, appendix: any): string {
    if (typeof appendix === "number") {
        return text + Array(appendix).join(" ");
    }
    if (typeof appendix === "string") {
        return text + appendix;
    }
    throw new Error("appendix must be string or number");
}
```

Listing 4.16: 04\10_unionTypes\starter\main.ts

When you call the function of listing 4.16 with a boolean as appendix, you get a runtime error:

```
append("Thomas", true); // Runtime-error
```

Now let's see how a union type can help here to produce a compile-time error for the code line above.

You know already that the appendix-parameter of the append-function should be either string or number. So instead of using the any-type, you should use the union type string | number.

Listing 4.17 shows the adjusted append-function. The union type string | number is used for the appendix-parameter. Using that union type also means that you don't have to throw an Error anymore if the appendix is neither string nor number, because now it will always be a string or a number.

```
function append(text: string, appendix: string | number): string {
    if (typeof appendix === "number") {
        return text + Array(appendix).join(" ");
    }
    if (typeof appendix === "string") {
        return text + appendix;
    }
    // Error not needed anymore, as code is never reached
    // throw new Error("appendix must be string or number");
}
```

Listing 4.17: 04\10_unionTypes\done\main.ts

With the adjusted `append`-function of listing 4.17, the line below leads to a compile-time error, as the value `true` is not assignable to a parameter of type `string | number`:

```
append("Thomas", true); // Compile-time-error
```

Returning Void

The type void is used as a return-type of a function. Void means the function returns no value. The `logIt`-function below just logs the input-string to the browser's console. Its return type is `void`.

```
function logIt(input: string): void {
  console.log(input);
}
```

The TypeScript compiler infers the return type of functions where it can. For the function above, you can omit the void-annotation. The TypeScript compiler will find out that there's no return-statement and infers that the return type is `void`.

Never

The type `never` is used for values that never occur. For example, a function that always throws an error has the return type `never`:

```
function doSomething(): never {
  throw new Error("Not implemented");
}
```

Never is also used for variables. Look at the function in listing 4.18.

```
function append(text: string, appendix: string | number): string {
    if (typeof appendix === "number") {
        return text + Array(appendix).join(" ");
    }
    if (typeof appendix === "string") {
        return text + appendix;
    }
    // Here appendix has the type never
}
```

Listing 4.18: appendix has the type never after the two if-statements

The appendix-parameter in listing 4.18 is defined as a union type `string | number`. If you try to use the `appendix`-parameter after the two `if`-statements, it has the type `never`. This is because the TypeScript compiler notices that this code is never reached. Yes, the compiler is smart.

Undefined, null and Strict Null Checking

Undefined and null are the values in JavaScript that lead to many errors. In TypeScript, these values have their own types: `undefined` and `null`. By default, `undefined` and `null` are subtypes of all other types in Typescript. That means for example, you can assign `null` or `undefined` to a `string`-variable:

```
let firstName: string = "Thomas";
firstName = null; // OK
firstName = undefined; // OK
```

As mentioned, `undefined` and `null` can lead to runtime-errors, as you might access members of a variable that is either `null` or `undefined`.

To prevent these errors, the TypeScript compiler has a strictNullChecks-option that is available since TypeScript 2.0. You can set it to `true` in your *tsconfig.json*-file like in listing 4.19.

```
{
    "compilerOptions": {
        "module": "commonjs",
        "target": "es5",
        "noImplicitAny": false,
        "sourceMap": false,
        "strictNullChecks": true
    }
}
```

Listing 4.19: 04\11_strictNullChecking\tsconfig.json

With the strictNullChecks-option turned on, the types `undefined` and `null` are no more subtypes of all other types. That means you can't assign them anymore for example to a string-variable:

```
let firstName: string = "Thomas";
firstName = null; // Error
firstName = undefined; // Error
```

If you want to use `null` or `undefined` with the strictNullChecks-option turned on, you have to explicitly specify them by using a union type. The code below shows this. The union type `string | null` allows strings and the value `null`, but you can't assign the value `undefined` to the variable, as that type is not part of the union type:

```typescript
let firstName: string | null = "Thomas";
firstName = null; // Ok
firstName = undefined; // Error
```

Listing 4.20: 04\11_strictNullChecking\main.ts

Summary

In this chapter, you learned about the basic types in TypeScript, like number, boolean and string. You also learned how the TypeScript compiler can infer types.

When you create an array, you can iterate over the values of that array with a for-of-loop. If you need a kind of fixed array with different types in it, you can use a tuple.

TypeScript supports enums. With an enum, you can give friendly names to a set of numbers.

When you need to run dynamic code that is not known at compile-time, you can use the `any`-type.

If you know better than the TypeScript compiler what kind of object a variable will contain at runtime, you can use a type assertion with the as-operator. Then you'll get statement completion and type checking on the members.

You learned in this chapter also about union types that allow you to combine some existing types to a new type. You also learned about TypeScript's `strictNullChecks`-option. When you set it to `true` in your *tsconfig.json*-file, you have to explicitly use union types for your variables if you want to assign the values `null` or `undefined` to them.

So far so good. You know already a lot about the basic types in TypeScript. Maybe you've noticed that the variables in this book are declared with the `let`-keyword. Let's look at this a bit more detailed before you learn about interfaces and classes.

5. Var, Let and Const

Introduction

Variables in JavaScript have always been declared with the `var`-keyword. But with ES2015, the new keywords `let` and `const` have been introduced, and of course these keywords are also available in TypeScript. It is recommended to use `let` and `const` instead of `var`.

In this chapter, you learn how to use `let` and `const` and you learn about the differences between `var`, `let` and `const`.

Declare Variables

Variable declarations with `let` and `const` are similar to variable declarations with `var`. Instead of using the var-keyword like here

```
var firstName: string = "Thomas"
```

you just use the `let` or `const` keyword

```
let firstName: string = "Thomas"
const nonChangeableFirstName: string = "Julia"
```

But what are the differences? Let's look at some differences between `var` and `let` before we look at `const`-variables.

Function-scoped vs. Block-scoped

Variables declared with the `var`-keyword are function-scoped. This leads to headaches for programmers with a C-style language background. Look at this function:

```
function getNumber(init) {
   if(init) {
      var x = 9;
   }
   return x;
}
```

Listing 5.1: *Using function-scoped variable with var*

In listing 5.1, the variable x is declared in an `if`-block and then used outside of that `if`-block. That's valid JavaScript, as `var`-variables are not block-scoped, but function-scoped. That means when you declare a `var`-variable in a function, you can access it from anywhere in that function. It doesn't matter if the declaration is inside of an `if`-block like in the function of listing 5.1.

Now let's change `var` to `let` like in listing 5.2. In contrast to `var`, `let`-variables are not function-scoped, but block-scoped. Now you'll get a compile-time error, as the variable x is not visible outside of the `if`-block where it is declared.

```
function getNumber(init) {
   if(init) {
      let x = 9;
   }
   return x; // Error: x not visible here, as "let" is block-scoped
}
```

Listing 5.2: Using block-scoped variable with let

Multiple Declarations

You can declare a variable with `var` multiple times. This is valid code:

```
var firstName: string = "Thomas";
var firstName: string = "Julia";
```

When you're using `let`, you can't declare the same variable in the same block-scope. If you do it, you get a compile-time error for each declaration that tells you that you cannot redeclare the block-scoped `firstName`-variable:

```
let firstName: string = "Thomas"; // Compile-time error
let firstName: string = "Julia"; // Compile-time error
```

But what is allowed with `let` is a concept called shadowing. That means you re-declare a variable in another block-scope like in the function of listing 5.3. The inner block redeclares the `firstName`-variable. That means it hides the variable from the outer-block, but it doesn't change it. It is a completely different variable in the inner scope that has a different value. After the inner scope, the variable-name `firstName` refers again to the outer variable.

```
let firstName: string = "Thomas";
{
   let firstName: string = "Bill";
   console.log(firstName); // Logs "Bill"
}
console.log(firstName); // Logs "Thomas"
```

Listing 5.3: *05\03_shadowing\main.ts*

> **Note**
> Re-declaring a variable with the same name in an inner block might confuse many developers. Instead of shadowing it's recommended to use another name for the variable in the inner block. That leads to better code readability and to more friends in the team you're working at.

Declare Before Access

Another rule of `let` is that the variable needs to be declared before you access it. That means this leads to an error:

```
console.log(firstName); // Error: firstName used before declaration
let firstName: string = "Thomas";
```

Not the line number of the declaration is important, but the flow how your code is executed. In the code snippet above, the `console.log`-call is executed before the declaration of the `firstName`-variable, so that leads to an error. But now look at the code of listing 5.4. The `log`-function is called after the `firstName`-declaration, so this is valid code that does not produce any errors.

```
function log() {
   console.log(firstName); // Ok to access firstName here
}
let firstName: string = "Thomas";
log();
```

Listing 5.4: *Variable is created before it is accessed*

Using Const

All the rules for `let` that you've seen in this chapter also apply to `const`. Like `let`-variables `const`-variables are block-scoped and not function-scoped. The only difference between `const` and `let` is that a `const`-variable can be assigned only once. And the assignment of a value needs to happen at its declaration.

That means whenever a variable shouldn't be re-assigned, you can use `const` instead of `let`. Look at the following statement. The `firstName`-variable cannot be re-assigned, as it is a `const`-variable.

```
const firstName: string = "Thomas";
firstName = "Julia"; // Error: firstName is a const
```

When you're assigning an object to a `const`-variable, you can still change the object's properties. But you can't re-assign a new object to the `const`-variable:

```
const friend = { firstName: "Thomas", lastName: "TypeScripter" };
friend.firstName = "Julia"; // OK
friend.lastName = "Huber"; // OK
friend = { firstName: "x", lastName: "y" }; // Error: friend is const
```

Summary

In this chapter, you learned about the keywords `let` and `const` that you use to declare variables in TypeScript. The classic `var`-keyword is still around in TypeScript, as TypeScript is a JavaScript superset. But you should always prefer `let` and `const`, that are also part of ES2015.

In contrast to `var`, `let` and `const` variables are not function-scoped, but block-scoped.

Now let's continue with interfaces and classes.

6. Interfaces and Classes

Introduction

With TypeScript, you can use object-oriented constructs like interfaces, classes and inheritance to build a robust code base. Classes are in the specification of ES2015, but interfaces are a concept only available in TypeScript.

In this chapter, you read how to use interfaces before you learn how to create and instantiate classes. You also learn about TypeScript's type compatibility, which is different from languages like C# or Java.

After that this chapter shows you how to set modifiers on class members to control access to these class members.

The next thing you learn are TypeScript's parameter properties – a shorthand syntax to create properties and constructor parameters in one go. You also learn how to create read only properties and how to create static properties.

When using classes, TypeScript also supports inheritance and abstract classes to build up a class hierarchy. You learn about these topics, and also how to use and extend base classes.

At the end of this chapter you learn how you can check the type of an object with the `instanceof`-operator, and you also read how you can destructure objects.

Alright? Let's begin with interfaces.

Interfaces

You've already used an interface in chapter 3, "Using TypeScript". An interface is a TypeScript construct. There's no compiled output in JavaScript. This is because an interface is just a type without implementation. As JavaScript has no types and as there is no implementation for an interface, there's nothing to generate in JavaScript.

An interface is used to create clean boundaries for your code. If you don't satisfy the interface, you get a compile-time error. Look at the `getFullName`-function in listing 6.1, there are no types defined. You can call the function and pass in whatever you want.

```
function getFullName(friend) {
    let fullName = friend.firstName;
    if(friend.lastName) {
        fullName += " " + friend.lastName;
    }
    return fullName;
}
```

Listing 6.1: a simple getFullName function

With an interface, you can restrict the type passed to the function of listing 6.1. What you can see in the function of listing 6.1 is that the `firstName`-property of a friend is required, and the `lastName`-property is optional.

With an interface, you can define optional members by using a question mark after the member-name. Look at the `lastName`-property in listing 6.2, it's optional.

```
interface Friend {
    firstName: string;
    lastName?: string;
}
```

Listing 6.2: 06\01_interfaces\main.ts

Now you can extend the `getFullName`-function with the new `Friend`-type like in listing 6.3.

```
function getFullName(friend: Friend): string {
    ...
}
```

Listing 6.3: 06\01_interfaces\main.ts

With the types in place, you get statement completion in Visual Studio Code when you call the `getFullName`-function. Visual Studio Code suggests the properties of the passed in object. You can omit the `lastName`-property as it is optional. But if you omit the required `firstName`-property, you get a compile-time error. Listing 6.4 shows this.

```
console.log(getFullName({firstName:"Thomas",lastName:"Huber"}));
console.log(getFullName({firstName:"Thomas"}));
console.log(getFullName({})); // Error: firstName is missing
```

Listing 6.4: 06\01_interfaces\main.ts

Create and Instantiate a Class

ES2015 has support for classes. With TypeScript, you can use classes and compile them down to ES5 or even ES3.

A class has typically properties, methods and a constructor that is used to create an instance of the class.

> Note: Class vs. Interface
>
> If you're not familiar with object-oriented principles: An interface has never an implementation, it's just a code contract. A class on the other side can have a constructor that executes code, methods that execute code, properties with accessors that execute code etc. So, if it's hard for you to decide whether to use an interface or a class, just ask yourself this question: Do I want to associate any logic with such an object? If yes, use a class. But if the answer is more "I just need to ensure that the members exist, it's a pure contract", then use an interface.

Listing 6.5 shows a `Friend`-class. It has the properties `firstName` and `lastName`. Note that the `lastName`-property is optional. The constructor creates a new instance of the class and initializes these two properties. With the keyword `this` the actual instance of the class is referenced. This is similar like in C# or Java. The `getFullName`-method returns the full name of a friend by using the properties `firstName` and `lastName`.

> Note: Method vs. Function
>
> The `Friend`-class of listing 6.5 has a `getFullName`-method. But why do we call this a method and not a function? In fact, it is of course a function. But we call it a method as it is a class-member. That's usually what object oriented vocabulary looks like. Classes have a constructor, properties, and methods.

```
class Friend {
    firstName: string;
    lastName?: string;

    constructor(firstName: string, lastName?: string) {
        this.firstName = firstName;
        this.lastName = lastName;
    }

    getFullName(): string {
        let fullName = this.firstName;
        if(this.lastName) {
            fullName+= " "+this.lastName;
        }
        return fullName;
    }
}
```

Listing 6.5: *06\02_classes\main.ts*

To instantiate a `Friend`-object, you use the `new`-keyword. This is similar like creating objects in C# or Java. You can omit the optional parameters of the constructor. The following code creates two `Friend`-objects:

```
let friend1 = new Friend("Thomas","Huber");
let friend2 = new Friend("Julia");
console.log(friend1.getFullName()); // Logs "Thomas Huber"
console.log(friend2.getFullName()); // Logs "Julia"
```

When you create a class in TypeScript, you should look at the generated JavaScript code for your learning experience. With ES5, you'll see JavaScript code that uses prototypes for methods. Listing 6.6 shows the compiled ES5-code from the `Friend`-class of listing 6.5.

```
var Friend = (function () {
    function Friend(firstName, lastName) {
        this.firstName = firstName;
        this.lastName = lastName;
    }
    Friend.prototype.getFullName = function () {
        var fullName = this.firstName;
        if (this.lastName) {
            fullName += " " + this.lastName;
        }
        return fullName;
    };
    return Friend;
}());
```

Listing 6.6: main.js-file compiled as ES5

Now go to your *tsconfig.json*-file and change the target-version to ES2015 or later, like you learned it in chapter 3, "Using TypeScript". Then you'll see that classes are a native part of JavaScript. The code in listing 6.7 is the generated JavaScript code out of listing 6.5 with ES2015 as target-version. It looks exactly like the TypeScript code, just without the type annotations.

```
class Friend {
    constructor(firstName, lastName) {
        this.firstName = firstName;
        this.lastName = lastName;
    }
    getFullName() {
        let fullName = this.firstName;
        if (this.lastName) {
            fullName += " " + this.lastName;
        }
        return fullName;
    }
}
```

Listing 6.7: main.js-file compiled as ES2015

Implement an Interface

Classes can implement one or more interfaces by using the `implements`-keyword. Let's assume you have a `Developer`-interface:

```
interface Developer {
    knowsTypeScript: boolean;
}
```

You can implement it on your `Friend`-class like this:

```
class Friend implements Developer {
    knowsTypeScript: boolean;
}
```

Implementing an interface on a class just ensures that the members of the interface exist in the class. But for type compatibility, implementing an interface is not necessary in TypeScript. This is different to languages like C# or Java. Let's look at what this means.

> **Note**
>
> To implement multiple interfaces on a class, you just separate them by using commas:
>
> ```
> class Friend implements Developer, Coder, Scripter {
>     ...
> }
> ```

Type Compatibility in TypeScript

To check type compatibility, TypeScript is using structural typing, and not nominal typing that is used in languages like C# and Java. Structural typing means that the members of an object are important, and not the type itself.

Let's assume you have the following `Developer`-interface that defines a `knowsTypeScript`-property:

```
interface Developer {
    knowsTypeScript: boolean;
}
```

Now you have a `Friend`-class that has exactly the same `knowsTypeScript`-property as defined in the `Developer`-interface, but note that the `Friend`-class does not implement the `Developer`-interface:

```
class Friend {
    knowsTypeScript: boolean;
}
```

As TypeScript is using structural typing, you can use a `Friend`, wherever a `Developer` is required, because the `Friend`-class has the required `knowsTypeScript`-property. That means this works:

```
let dev: Developer = new Friend(); // OK, because member exists
```

Access Modifiers of Class Members

All members of a class, like properties, methods and the constructor are by default public in TypeScript. That means this `firstName`-property is public:

```
class Friend {
    firstName: string;
}
```

Public means you can access the property from outside of the class, like here in this code statement that is not in the `Friend`-class:

```
let friend = new Friend();
friend.firstName = "Thomas ";
```

You can also be explicit and mark your property as public:

```
class Friend {
    public firstName: string;
}
```

Beside `public`, TypeScript has two other access modifiers:

- `private` – member is only visible inside of the class, not from outside
- `protected` – member is only visible inside of the class and in subclasses, but not from outside

Look at the `Friend`-class below. The `firstName`-property is private. You can only access it inside of the class with `this.firstName`:

```
class Friend {
    private firstName: string;

    constructor (firstName: string) {
        this.firstName = firstName;
    }
}
```

When you try to access the `firstName`-property from outside of the class, you get an error, as it is private.

```
let friend = new Friend("Thomas");
let firstName = friend.firstName; // Error, firstName is private
```

Parameter Properties

Parameter Properties are a short-hand syntax of TypeScript to create properties that are initialized from constructor parameters. Let's look at the `Friend`-class of listing 6.8. The `firstName`-property is initialized from a constructor-parameter that has the same name as the property.

```
class Friend {
    firstName: string;

    constructor(firstName: string) {
        this.firstName = firstName;
    }
}
```

Listing 6.8: *firstName-property is initialized in the constructor*

Instead of explicitly defining the `firstName`-property and initialize it in the constructor – like it's done in listing 6.8, you can use parameter properties. Just add modifiers to your constructor parameters, and the TypeScript compiler generates the properties behind the scenes and initializes them in the constructor. Look at the class of listing 6.9. It is equal to the class of listing 6.8.

```
class Friend {
    constructor(public firstName: string) { }
}
```

Listing 6.9: *06\04_parameterProperties\main.ts*

The constructor parameter in listing 6.9 has a public modifier. This tells the TypeScript compiler to create a property with the same name as the parameter. The TypeScript compiler will also initialize the generated property from the value of the constructor parameter. That's why this concept is called parameter properties: A property is created and initialized from a constructor parameter.

All you need to do is adding a modifier to your constructor parameter: `public`, `protected` or `private`. That's it.

When you go back to listing 6.5 where we created the bigger `Friend`-class with the properties `firstName` and `lastName` and the `getFullName`-method, you can write that class also shorter with parameter properties. Listing 6.10 shows it. The properties `firstName` and `lastName` are created from the constructor parameters, because the parameters have the `public` access modifier.

```
class Friend {
    constructor(public firstName: string,
                public lastName?: string) { }

    getFullName(): string {
        let fullName = this.firstName;
        if(this.lastName) {
            fullName+= " "+this.lastName;
        }
        return fullName;
    }
}
```

Listing 6.10: *Friend class using parameter properties*

Readonly Properties

You can define a readonly property with the `readonly`-keyword. A readonly property must be initialized either at its declaration or in the constructor. At other places, you can't assign a new value.

The Friend-class in listing 6.11 has a `firstName`-property that is readonly.

```
class Friend {
    public readonly firstName: string;

    constructor(firstName: string) {
        this.firstName = firstName;
    }
}
```

Listing 6.11: Friend-class with readonly property

You can also use the `readonly`-keyword on a parameter property. The class in listing 6.12 is the same as the class in listing 6.11.

```
class Friend {
    constructor(public readonly firstName: string) { }
}
```

Listing 6.12: 06\05_readonlyProperties\main.ts

> **Note**
>
> As `public` is the default modifier for class members, you could even omit the `public` keyword in listing 6.12. The `readonly`-keyword would be enough for the TypeScript compiler to know that this is a parameter property.

With the readonly-property in place, you can only read the property, but not write to it anymore, as listing 6.13 shows.

```
let friend = new Friend("Thomas");
console.log(friend.firstName); // OK
friend.firstName = "Julia"; // Error, as it is readonly
```

Listing 6.13: 06\05_readonlyProperties\main.ts

The readonly keyword can also be used on interfaces:

```
interface Developer {
    readonly knowsTypeScript: boolean;
}
```

Listing 6.14: 06\05_readonlyProperties\main.ts

Then you can't change the value of that readonly property after you've assigned an object to a variable of that interface. Listing 6.15 shows this behaviour.

```
let dev: Developer = {knowsTypeScript:true};
console.log(dev.knowsTypeScript); // OK
dev.knowsTypeScript = false; // Error, as it is readonly
```

Listing 6.15: 06\05_readonlyProperties\main.ts

Properties with Accessors

If you're familiar with C#, you know the accessors get and set that are used to access a property. TypeScript has a similar concept with set and get accessors. They're great if you need to know when a property is read or written. You can just hook in some extra code.

Listing 6.16 shows a Friend-class with a firstName-property. There's a private field _firstName that stores the value. Then there's the set-accessor for the firstName-property. It looks pretty much like a method that has a value-parameter of type string. Inside of the set-accessor, the private _firstName field is set to the received value. There's also a get-accessor that returns the value of the _firstName field. It's not hard to imagine how you can put additional code into the set- or get-accessor.

```
class Friend {
    private _firstName: string;
    set firstName(value: string)     {
        this._firstName = value;
    }
    get firstName(): string {
        return this._firstName;
    }
}
```

Listing 6.16: 06\06_propertyAccessors\main.ts

When you use the Friend-class of listing 6.16, it feels like it has a plain firstName-property. That means the get- and set-accessors are not visible outside of the class, they're an internal thing. The snippet below shows this.

```
let friend = new Friend();
friend.firstName = "Thomas"; // feels like a plain property
console.log(friend.firstName);
```

You can also build a class that has just a `get`-accessor for a property, but no `set`-accessor. If you do this, the property is readonly for the code outside of this class. But inside of the class, you can still change the underlying field where you store the value for the property.

Look at the `Friend`-class below, it has only a `get`-accessor for the `firstName`-property:

```
class Friend {
    private _firstName: string = "Thomas";
    get firstName(): string {
        return this._firstName;
    }
}
```

Inside of the `Friend`-class above you can still modify the underlying `_firstName`-field. But from outside of the class, you can only read the `firstName`-property. When you try to set it, the TypeScript compiler gives you an error that tells you that the `firstName`-property is readonly.

```
let friend = new Friend();
console.log(friend.firstName); // OK
friend.firstName = "Julia"; // Error, as property is readonly
```

Static Properties

TypeScript supports static properties. Static properties belong to the class, and not to an instance of a class. That means their value exists just once, no matter how many instances you create of the class.

Listing 6.17 defines a static `friendCounter`-property in the `Friend`-class. It is initialized with the value zero. In the constructor, the property is incremented by one.

```
class Friend {
    static friendCounter: number = 0;

    constructor() {
        Friend.friendCounter++;
    }
}
```

Listing 6.17: 06\07_staticProperties\main.ts

Listing 6.18 creates three `Friend`-objects. After that the value of the static `friendCounter`-property is logged to the console. It has the value three.

```
new Friend();
new Friend();
new Friend();
console.log(Friend.friendCounter); // Logs 3
```

Listing 6.18: 06\07_staticProperties\main.ts

Inheritance

TypeScript supports inheritance. You can use the `extends`-keyword to extend an existing class. Listing 6.19 contains a `Friend`-class with a `firstName`-property. The `Developer`-class inherits from the `Friend`-class.

```
class Friend {
    constructor(public firstName: string) { }
}
class Developer extends Friend {
    knowsTypeScript: boolean;
}
```

Listing 6.19: 06\08_inheritance\main.ts

Now a developer has a `firstName`-property inherited from the `Friend`-class and a `knowsTypeScript`-property that the `Developer`-class has defined. In listing 6.20 a developer is created and used.

```
let dev = new Developer("Thomas");
dev.knowsTypeScript = true;

console.log(dev.firstName);
console.log(dev.knowsTypeScript);
```

Listing 6.20: 06\08_inheritance\main.ts

When you look at the code of listing 6.20, you might notice that the constructor of the `Friend`-class is used to create a developer. The constructor of the `Friend`-class takes the firstname as a parameter. But maybe you want to have your own constructor in the `Developer`-class. You can do this. There's just one rule: When you define a constructor in a subclass, you need to call the base-class constructor by using the `super`-keyword.

Listing 6.21 shows a new `Developer`-class that has its own constructor. In that constructor, the constructor of the base-class is called by using `super`.

```
class Friend {
    constructor(public firstName: string) { }
}
class Developer extends Friend {
    constructor(firstName: string, public knowsTypeScript: boolean) {
        super(firstName);
    }
}
```

Listing 6.21: 06\08_inheritance\main.ts

With the new constructor, a `Developer` is instantiated like this:

```
var dev = new Developer("Thomas",true);
```

Abstract Classes

TypeScript supports the concept of abstract classes. With an abstract class, you force a subclass to implement the abstract members. To create an abstract class, you mark the class with the `abstract` keyword. Members that need to be implemented by a subclass get the `abstract` keyword as well. They have no implementation in your abstract base-class.

Listing 6.22 shows the abstract `Friend`-class. The `sayHello`-method is marked as abstract. Note that it has no method-body. The implementation needs to be done by the subclasses.

```
abstract class Friend {
    constructor(public firstName: string) { }

    abstract sayHello(): void;
}
```

Listing 6.22: 06\09_abstractClasses\main.ts

Listing 6.23 shows a `Developer`-class that extends the abstract `Friend`-class. It implements the `sayHello`-method and logs a message to the console by using the `firstName`-property that is inherited from the Friend-class.

```
class Developer extends Friend {
    knowsTypeScript: boolean;

    sayHello() {
        console.log(`Hi, I'm ${this.firstName}`)
    }
}
```

Listing 6.23: 06\09_abstractClasses\main.ts

Now the developer can be created and used like any other class:

```
var dev = new Developer("Thomas");
dev.sayHello(); // Logs "Hi, I'm Thomas" to the console
```

Constructor Parameters

TypeScript allows only one constructor per class. You can't define multiple constructors like for example in C#. But with optional parameters and default values for parameters, you can decide what parameters are necessary to create an object of your class.

Let's assume you have this `Friend`-class with a `firstName`-property:

```
class Friend {
    constructor(public firstName: string) { }
}
```

Now you can instantiate a new `Friend` by passing a string to the constructor, but you can't instantiate a new `Friend` without passing a string:

```
let friend1 = new Friend("Thomas");
let friend2 = new Friend(); // Error: Parameter is missing
```

Now let's make the `firstName`-property optional:

```
class Friend {
    constructor(public firstName?: string) { }
}
```

With the optional `firstName`-property, you can instantiate a new `Friend` without passing a string to the constructor:

```
let friend1 = new Friend("Thomas");
let friend2 = new Friend(); // OK, as firstName is optional
```

Instead of setting the `firstName` to optional, you could also define a default value for it. This snippet defines the default value "Julia":

```
class Friend {
    constructor(public firstName: string = "Julia") { }
}
```

With a default-value defined, you can call the constructor without passing in a string:

```
let friend = new Friend();
console.log(friend.firstName); // Logs "Julia"
```

The instanceof Operator

Sometimes you need to find out what kind of object you're working with at runtime. Let's assume you have this little class-hierarchy of listing 6.24.

```
class Friend {
    constructor(public firstName: string) { }
}
class Developer extends Friend {
    knowsTypeScript: boolean;
}
class ExcelGuru extends Friend{ }
```

Listing 6.24: 06\11_instanceOf\main.ts

Now let's assign a `Developer` to a `friend`-variable:

```
let friend: Friend = new Developer("Thomas");
```

Now let's imagine you don't know that the `friend`-variable contains a `Developer`. Maybe because the user can dynamically select Developers and Excel Gurus in your app, and you handle all those objects in a single array of type `Friend[]`. In your code, you might want to find out if the selected `Friend` is a `Developer` if you want to access its `knowsTypeScript`-property. And to find this out, you use the `instanceof` operator.

Listing 6.25 shows how the `instanceof` operator is used. The `if`-statement checks if the `friend`-variable contains a `Developer`-instance by using the `instanceof` operator. Then the code can access the developers `knowsTypeScript`-property.

```
if(friend instanceof Developer) {
    console.log("Yeah, it's a dev");
    console.log("Knows TypeScript: "+friend.knowsTypeScript)
}
```

Listing 6.25: 06\11_instanceOf\main.ts

But wait: We access the `knowsTypeScript`-property without using a type assertion? Shouldn't it be like

```
(friend as Developer).knowsTypeScript
```

No, we don't have to use a type assertion here. When we are inside of the `if`-statement in listing 6.25, the TypeScript compiler knows that the `friend`-variable contains a `Developer`, because we checked it in the `if`-statement with the `instanceof`-operator. Yes, the TypeScript compiler is a clever beast.

Destructuring Objects

Sometimes you want to extract single properties from an object. For example, if a method returns a complex object, but you just need a single property of that object. Wouldn't it be great to grab just the value you need?

ES2015 and so TypeScript support exactly this: You can extract one or more properties from an object, and this feature is called destructuring. Let's take the `Friend`-class of listing 6.26 to learn how destructuring works.

```
class Friend {
    constructor(public firstName: string,
        public lastName: string,
        public isDeveloper: boolean) { }
}
```

Listing 6.26: 06\12_desctructuring\main.ts

Let's assume you have a `Friend`-object created like this:

```
let friend = new Friend("Thomas","Huber",true);
```

Now let's assume you don't need the `firstName`-property in your code, and you want to store the value of the `lastName`-property in a variable called `surname` and the value of the `isDeveloper`-property in a variable called `isDev`. You can do this the classic way like in listing 6.27.

```
let surname = friend.lastName;
let isDev = friend.isDeveloper;
```

Listing 6.27: Extracting two properties the classic way

Instead of extracting the two properties the classic way, you can use a destructuring like shown in listing 6.28. It stores the `lastName`-property like in listing 6.27 in a `surname`-variable, and the `isDeveloper`-property in an `isDev`-variable.

```
let {lastName: surname, isDeveloper: isDev} = friend;
console.log(surname);
console.log(isDev);
```

Listing 6.28: 06\12_desctructuring\main.ts

If you want that the created variables have the same name as the properties, the destructuring can be written like in listing 6.29.

```
let {lastName, isDeveloper} = friend;
console.log(lastName);
console.log(isDeveloper);
```

Listing 6.29: 06\12_desctructuring\main.ts

Now when you think about functions that are returning an object, and your code just needs a subset of the properties of the returned object, then destructuring is quite powerful. Let's take the `loadFriend`-method of listing 6.30 as an example.

```
function loadFriend(): Friend {
    return new Friend("Julia", "Huber", false);
}
```

Listing 6.30: 06\12_desctructuring\main.ts

If you need just the `firstName`-property of the `Friend`-object returned by the `loadFriend`-method, you can destructure the return value like in listing 6.31 into a `firstName`-variable.

```
let {firstName} = loadFriend();
console.log(firstName);
```

Listing 6.31: 06\12_desctructuring\main.ts

If you need more properties like for example the `lastName`, you just add them to the destructuring:

```
let {firstName, lastName} = loadFriend();
```

Note that this works on a single line of code. Isn't this beautiful?!

> **Note**
>
> Beside destructuring objects like shown in this section you can also destructure arrays with TypeScript. Let's assume you have defined this number-array:
> ```
> let numbers: number[] = [1,2,3,4];
> ```
> Then you can destructure for example the first two values into variables with the names `first` and `second` like this:
> ```
> let [first, second] = numbers;
> console.log(first); // logs 1
> console.log(second); // logs 2
> ```

Summary

In this chapter, you learned about interfaces and classes. An interface is used for type-checking and tooling support. It does not have any implementation, and so there's no output in the compiled JavaScript code for an interface.

On the other side, classes can contain logic. They have properties, methods and a constructor. Classes are a native part of ES2015. With TypeScript, you can use classes like in ES2015 and compile your code down to ES5 or even ES3.

You learned that class members like properties, methods and constructors are public by default. You can set them to private if you don't want them to be accessible from outside of the class. You can also set them to protected if you want them to be accessible from subclasses, but not from outside of the class.

One of the great features of TypeScript are parameter properties. When you define an access modifier like public, protected or private on a constructor parameter, TypeScript will generate and initialize a property with the same name behind the scenes for you. That's a powerful short-hand syntax.

Beside all that you learned about inheritance, abstract classes and the great `instanceof`-operator that allows you to check for a specific type in your code. You also learned the basics about extracting properties from objects by using destructuring.

In the next chapter, you read more about interfaces and classes when we look at generics! Are you ready? Let's go!

7. Generics

Introduction

All developers try to build re-usable components, and generics that are supported in TypeScript are a great way to do this.

Most often a re-usable component is born due to some refactoring. Let's assume you write a class called `NumberList`. The intention of this class is a list that only allows numbers. The next day you write a `StringList`-class that has exactly the same logic, but allows only strings. With generics, you can refactor the two classes into a single class called `List<T>`. The T-parameter – also called generic type parameter - allows you to specify the type you want to use with the class. You can instantiate a `List<number>` or a `List<string>` or even something totally different like a `List<Friend>`.

> **Note**
> `List<string>` is spoken as "List of string".

If you know a language like C# or Java, you might already be familiar with generics. The concepts in TypeScript are quite similar to these languages.

In this chapter, you read how to define generic functions, generic interfaces and generic classes in TypeScript. You also learn how to define constraints on the generic type parameter. But first, let's look at the generic `Array<T>` type.

The Generic Array Type

In chapter 4, "Basic Types", you learned that there are two ways to define the type of an array:

```
let firstNames: string[] = ["Thomas", "Sara", "Julia"];
let firstNames: Array<string> = ["Thomas", "Sara", "Julia"];
```

As you can see, TypeScript has a generic `Array<T>` type. You can also call the `Array<T>` constructor like in Listing 7.1 to define a number array. If you try to push a string into the array, you get a compile-time error that the string is not assignable to a number.

```
let array = new Array<number>();
array.push(1);
array.push(2);
array.push("Hello"); // Error, string not assignable to number
```

Listing 7.1: 07\01_genericArray\main.ts

You can use all this generic functionality to create your own functions, interfaces and classes. Let's start with functions.

Generic Functions

To define a generic function, you specify a generic type parameter in angle brackets behind the function-name like in listing 7.2. The generic type parameter has usually the name T, but of course you can choose another name. The logToConsole-function of listing 7.2 has an item-parameter of type T and also a return-value of type T. The function just logs the passed in item to the console and returns it.

```
function logToConsole<T>(item: T): T {
  console.log(item);
  return item;
}
```

Listing 7.2: 07\02_genericFunctions\main.ts

When you call the generic logToConsole-function, you can specify the type and pass in a value of that type. In the code line below a string is used. Note that the function also returns a string.

```
let firstname: string = logToConsole<string>("Thomas");
```

The TypeScript compiler is even clever enough to infer the generic type you want to use with the logToConsole-function by looking at the type of the passed in value. When you pass in a string, the compiler knows it must be logToConsole<string>, when you pass in a number, the compiler knows it must be logToConsole<number>. That's the reason why you can omit the type, and you still get the correct type back from the function:

```
let firstname: string = logToConsole("Thomas");
let luckyNumber: number = logToConsole(13);
```

Listing 7.3: 07\02_genericFunctions\main.ts

Generic Interfaces

Like on a function, you can also specify a generic type parameter on an interface. Listing 7.4 shows the generic `IRepository<T>`-interface. The `getAll`-method returns an array of the specified type, and the `insert`-method takes an item of the specified type.

```
interface IRepository<T> {
  getAll(): T[];
  insert(item: T): void;
}
```

Listing 7.4: 07\03_genericInterfaces\main.ts

Listing 7.5 shows a class that implements the `IRepository<Friend>`-interface. Internally the class uses an array to store the friends.

```
class FriendRepo implements IRepository<Friend> {
  private _items = new Array<Friend>();
  getAll() {
    return this._items;
  }
  insert(item: Friend): void {
    this._items.push(item);
  }
}
```

Listing 7.5: 07\03_genericInterfaces\main.ts

The `Friend`-class that is used in listing 7.5 has just a `firstName`-property:

```
class Friend {
  constructor(public firstName: string) { }
}
```

Listing 7.6: 07\03_genericInterfaces\main.ts

Listing 7.7 shows how the `FriendRepo`-class is used. Three friends are added to the `FriendRepo`, then the `getAll`-method is called to loop over the friends and log their firstnames to the console.

```
let repo = new FriendRepo();
repo.insert(new Friend("Thomas"));
repo.insert(new Friend("Julia"));
repo.insert(new Friend("Anna"));

for(let friend of repo.getAll())
{
  console.log(friend.firstName);
}
```

Listing 7.7: 07\03_genericInterfaces\main.ts

Generic Classes

When you look at the `FriendRepo`-class of listing 7.8, it might be obvious to your eyes – if you have used generics before - that you could refactor that code into a generic class. Then you can use the class with different types, and not only with friends.

```
class FriendRepo implements IRepository<Friend> {
  private _items = new Array<Friend>();
  getAll() {
    return this._items;
  }
  insert(item: Friend): void {
    this._items.push(item);
  }
}
```

Listing 7.8: 07\03_genericInterfaces\main.ts

To create a generic class, you specify the generic type parameter like on a function or on an interface within angle brackets after the class name.

Listing 7.9 shows the refactoring of listing 7.8. The `GenericRepo<T>`-class implements the interface `IRepository<T>`. The internally used array has also the generic type, and the `insert`-method takes an item of the generic type.

```
class GenericRepo<T> implements IRepository<T> {
  private _items = new Array<T>();
  getAll() {
    return this._items;
  }
  insert(item: T): void {
    this._items.push(item);
  }
}
```

Listing 7.9: 07\04_genericClasses\main.ts

With the generic class from listing 7.9 you can create for example a repo for numbers or for any other type you like:

```
let numberRepo = new GenericRepo<number>();
```

You can also create a repo for friends. All you need to do is specifying the type when you create the `GenericRepo`-instance:

```
let repo = new GenericRepo<Friend>();
repo.insert(new Friend("Thomas"));
repo.insert(new Friend("Julia"));
repo.insert(new Friend("Anna"));

for(let friend of repo.getAll())
{
  console.log(friend.firstName);
}
```

Listing 7.10: 07\04_genericClasses\main.ts

Generic Constraints

Sometimes you require some properties on a generic type. Let's assume you have created a `getById`-method in your `GenericRepo<T>`-class like shown in listing 7.11. When you access the `id`-property on the generic typed items, you get an error, as they don't have an id. But it's clear that your `getById`-method and so your `GenericRepo<T>`-class only works with types that have an `id`-property. To force that `id`-property to be available on the items, you can use generic constraints.

Chapter 7, "Generics"

```
class GenericRepo<T> {
  private _items = new Array<T>();
  getById(id: number) {
    return this._items.filter(item => item.id === id)[0];
  }
  ...
}
```

Listing 7.11: *The id on the generic type is not available*

First you need to define an interface. Listing 7.12 shows the simple interface `IHaveId` that defines the `id`-property.

```
interface IHaveId {
  id: number;
}
```

Listing 7.12: *07\05_genericConstraints\main.ts*

With the interface defined, you can use it on the generic type parameter with the `extends`-keyword like in listing 7.13.

```
class GenericRepo<T extends IHaveId> {
  private _items = new Array<T>();
  getById(id: number) {
    return this._items.filter(item => item.id === id)[0];
  }
  ...
}
```

Listing 7.13: *07\05_genericConstraints\main.ts*

Now the `GenericRepo<T>`-class only works with types that have an `id`-property, like for example the `Friend`-class of listing 7.14.

```
class Friend {
  constructor(public readonly id: number,
    public firstName: string) { }
}
```

Listing 7.14: *07\05_genericConstraints\main.ts*

As TypeScript is using structural typing, the `Friend`-class does not need to implement the `IHaveId`-interface. Having the `id`-property is sufficient to use the class where the `IHaveId`-interface is required. So, now you can create a `GenericRepo<Friend>`.

Multiple Type Parameters

When you define a generic function, interface or class, you can also define multiple generic type parameters. Just separate them with a comma. Listing 7.15 shows the generic `Dictionary`-class that has two generic type-parameters. It has the two methods `getItem` and `add`. Behind the scenes, the class stores the items in an array of tuples. The tuple is defined as [TKey, TValue].

```
class Dictionary<TKey, TValue> {
  private _items = new Array<[TKey, TValue]>();
  getItem(key: TKey): TValue {
    let foundItems = this._items.filter(item => item[0] == key);
    if(foundItems.length!=1)
    {
      throw new Error("Item with key does not exist");
    }
    return foundItems[0][1]; // Grab the tuple ([0]) and
                             // then the value ([1])
  }
  add(key: TKey, value: TValue): void {
    let keyExists
      = this._items.filter(item => item[0] == key).length > 0;
    if (keyExists) {
      throw new Error("Key exists already");
    }
    this._items.push([key, value]);
  }
}
```

Listing 7.15: 07\06_multipleTypeParameters\main.ts

Listing 7.16 shows how the dictionary of listing 7.15 is used. A new instance is created with the types `number` and `string`. Then three items are added. Then the `getItem`-method is called with the number 2, which returns the string Julia.

In the last statement of listing 7.16, the `add`-method is called with a `number` and a `boolean`. As the dictionary has been created with the types `number` and `string`, this leads to an error. The value `true` is not assignable to a string.

```
var dict = new Dictionary<number,string>();
dict.add(1,"Thomas");
dict.add(2,"Julia");
dict.add(3,"Anna");

let firstName:string= dict.getItem(2);
console.log(firstName); // Logs "Julia"

dict.add(4, true); // Error: true not assignable to string
```

Listing 7.16: 07\06_multipleTypeParameters\main.ts

Summary

In this chapter, you learned about generics. Generics are a great way to structure and re-use a lot of your code.

With TypeScript, you can define generic functions, generic interfaces and generic classes. The generic type parameters are defined in angle brackets after the name of your function, interface or class.

In this chapter, you got already a bit in touch with functions. Now let's look a bit more detailed at how functions are used and work in TypeScript.

8. Functions

Introduction

Functions are the key in TypeScript to execute some logic. You learn in this chapter about the types of functions in JavaScript, before we look at functions in TypeScript with optional parameters, default values and rest parameters.

You learn how to pass a function as a parameter to another function and how to define an interface for a function.

When it comes to functions, the `this`-keyword is quite important, it has usually the context of the function, but what is it pointing to when you use a function inside of a class? Is it the class-instance or the function? You learn about `this` and functions, and also about arrow functions that solve the `this`-problem.

The last thing you learn in this chapter are asynchronous functions in TypeScript with the keywords `async` and `await`. If you're a C# programmer, this last section with `async` and `await` might look quite familiar to you.

Ok, ready to dive in? Let's go.

Types of Functions in JavaScript

JavaScript supports two types of functions:
- Named functions
- Anonymous functions

The following snippet shows a named function. After the function-keyword, but before the parentheses is the name `multiply`.

```
function multiply(x, y) {
    return x * y;
}
```

The following line shows an anonymous function.

```
let add = function(x, y) { return x + y; };
```

An anonymous function has no name after the function keyword. But you can assign an anonymous function to a variable. When you do this, you can call it exactly like a named function via the name of the variable:

```
let resultMul = multiply(3, 3);
let resultAdd = add(3, 3);
```

Adding Types to Functions

With TypeScript, you can add types to functions. The anonymous function below has two `number`-parameters and a `number`-return value:

```
let add = function(x: number, y: number): number {return x + y;};
```

TypeScript infers the type of the `add`-variable in the line above. But you can also be explicit with a type annotation:

```
let add: (a: number, b: number) => number
    = function(x: number, y: number): number { return x + y; };
```

Note that the type annotation for a function is using the arrow-operator `=>` to define the return value, and not a colon like on the function itself.

Optional Parameters

In JavaScript, you can just omit parameters when calling a function. In TypeScript, you can't. But when you define a function, you can make a parameter optional by using a question mark after the parameter name. The `getFullName`-method in listing 8.1 has an optional `lastName`-parameter

```
function getFullName(firstName: string, lastName?: string) {
    if (lastName)
        return `${firstName} ${lastName}`;
    else
        return firstName;
}
```

Listing 8.1: 08\01_optionalParameters\main.ts

Now you can call this `getFullName`-method with two strings, with one string, but not without a string. The firstname is required. Listing 8.2 shows the possibilities

```
console.log(getFullName("Thomas", "Huber"));
console.log(getFullName("Thomas"));
console.log(getFullName()); // Error: firstName parameter missing
```

Listing 8.2: 08\01_optionalParameters\main.ts

> **Note**
> All required parameters of a function need to be defined before all the optional parameters.

Default Values

There are situations where you want to define a default value for a parameter. Then the caller doesn't have to pass in a value for that parameter. Look at the getFullName-method in listing 8.3. It's exactly the same method as in listing 8.1, with the only difference that it has a default-value for the required firstName-parameter.

```
function getFullName(firstName: string = "Julia", lastName?: string) {
    if (lastName)
        return `${firstName} ${lastName}`;
    else
        return firstName;
}
```

Listing 8.3: 08\02_defaultValues\main.ts

As a default-value is defined for the required firstName-parameter, you can call the method without passing in any value. The call below logs the default value Julia.

```
console.log(getFullName()); // OK, logs "Julia"
```

Rest Parameters

Sometimes you want to allow the caller of your function to pass in a variable number of arguments. TypeScript allows you to do this by defining rest parameters. Look at the `getFullName`-function in listing 8.4. The second parameter is called `moreNames`, and it is a `string`-array. Note that the `moreNames`-parameter has three leading dots: This is how you define a rest parameter.

```
function getFullName(firstName: string, ...moreNames: string[]) {
    return firstName + " " + moreNames.join(" ");
}
```

Listing 8.4: 08\03_restParameters\main.ts

With the rest parameter of listing 8.4, you can call the `getFullName`-function with as many strings as you want. Listing 8.5 shows some samples.

```
console.log(getFullName("Thomas"));
console.log(getFullName("Thomas", "Huber"));
console.log(getFullName("Thomas", "Claudius", "Huber"));
console.log(getFullName("Thomas", "Claudius", "Huber", "Developer"));
```

Listing 8.5: 08\03_restParameters\main.ts

Note that we don't pass in an array to the `getFullName`-function in listing 8.5. We use the function as it would have many string parameters. That's the power of rest parameters in TypeScript.

But you might find situations where you have an existing array that you want to pass to your function instead of separate rest parameters. To do this, you need to add three dots like in listing 8.6 in front of your argument.

```
let additionalNames: string[]= ["Claudius", "Huber", "Developer"];
console.log(getFullName("Thomas", ...additionalNames));
```

Listing 8.6: 08\03_restParameters\main.ts

Functions as Parameters

In JavaScript and so in TypeScript, you can have functions as parameters. This is used quite often when you have some kind of callback function. The `DataLoader`-class in listing 8.7 has a `loadAdminName`-method that has a `callback`-parameter. The `callback`-parameter's type is a function that has a `string`-parameter and returns `void`. In the body of the `loadAdminName`-method the callback is called immediately with the string Thomas.

```
class DataLoader {
    loadAdminName(callback: (adminName: string) => void) {
        callback("Thomas");
    }
}
```

Listing 8.7: 08\04_functionsAsParameters\main.ts

> **Note**
> Try to imagine that the `loadAdminName`-function of listing 8.7 does a http-call to get the admin name, and then it calls the callback function with that received admin name. This would be a real-life scenario. But to learn the concepts around functions in this chapter, we keep it simple and call the callback immediately with the hard-coded string `Thomas`.

Listing 8.8 shows how the `DataLoader`-class of listing 8.7 is used. An instance of the class is created and stored in the `loader`-variable. Then the `loadAdminName`-method is called. As an argument, a callback-function is passed in. The function has a string parameter like it is required by the parameter-type of the `loadAdminName`-method. The callback-function logs the received string to the browser's console.

```
let loader = new DataLoader();
loader.loadAdminName(function (loadedName: string) {
    console.log(loadedName); // Logs "Thomas"
})
```

Listing 8.8: 08\04_functionsAsParameters\main.ts

As we call the callback in listing 8.7 with the string Thomas, listing 8.8 logs exactly that string to the console.

Interfaces for Functions

When you use functions as parameters in other functions, your code might get a bit hard to read. Listing 8.9 shows the `DataLoader`-class of the previous section. The `loadAdminName`-method has a callback-parameter, its type is a very simple function that has a `string`-parameter and returns void. But it is already a bit hard to read, as you need to look exactly to see what's a parameter of the callback-function and what's a parameter of the `loadAdminName`-method. Now imagine if the callback would have for example five parameters instead of just one, then it would be even worse to read.

```
class DataLoader {
    loadAdminName(callback: (adminName: string) => void) {
        callback("Thomas");
    }
}
```

Listing 8.9: 08\05_interfacesForFunctions\main.ts

To make your code more readable when you have functions as parameters, you can use interfaces for your function types. In chapter 6, "Interfaces and Classes", we have defined interfaces for objects, but not for functions. Listing 8.10 shows the `AdminNameCallback`-interface. It contains a type-definition for a function that has a `string`-parameter and returns void. In contrast to an interface that you use for objects, where you would have methods and properties, there's no name in front of the function in listing 8.10. This makes this interface a pure interface that can be used for the defined function type.

```
interface AdminNameCallback {
    (adminName: string) : void
}
```

Listing 8.10: 08\05_interfacesForFunctions\main.ts

Listing 8.11 shows the adjusted `DataLoader`-class that is using the new `AdminNameCallback`-interface. The readability is a lot better, and the functionality is exactly the same as before.

```
class DataLoader {
    loadAdminName(callback:AdminNameCallback) {
        callback("Thomas");
    }
}
```

Listing 8.11: 08\05_interfacesForFunctions\main.ts

Functions and This

When you use functions in your classes, you need to be aware what the this-keyword is pointing to. Let's take our well-known DataLoader-class:

```
class DataLoader {
    loadAdminName(callback: AdminNameCallback) {
        callback("Thomas");
    }
}
```

Listing 8.12: 08\06_functionsAndThis\main.ts

Now let's assume you have written the AdminController-class of listing 8.13 that takes a DataLoader-instance as constructor parameter and stores it in the private dataLoader-property.

```
class AdminController {
    private _adminName:string;

    constructor(private dataLoader: DataLoader) { }

    get adminName():string { return this._adminName; }

    loadName() {
        this.dataLoader.loadAdminName(function (loadedName) {
            this._adminName = loadedName;
        })
    }
}
```

Listing 8.13: 08\06_functionsAndThis\main.ts

The AdminController-class has a private _adminName-field and a public get accessor that returns that field. In the loadName-method this _adminName-field is set. To set the field, the loadAdminName-method of the DataLoader-instance is called, and in the passed-in callback-function the `_adminName`-field is set to the loaded name. We refer to the `_adminName`-field by using the `this`-keyword.

If you are a C# or Java programmer, you might be pretty sure that `this` in listing 8.13 points to your `AdminController`-instance. But it's not true for the callback-function inside of the `loadName`-method. In listing 8.13 we refer to the `_adminName`-field by using the `this`-keyword, but `this` is used in the context of the function, it doesn't point to the `AdminController`-instance. That means the `_adminName`-field is not found on `this`.

You can see that problem in action when you instantiate a new `AdminController` like in listing 8.14. Just access the `adminName`-property after you have called the `loadName`-method. The `adminName`-property does not contain the expected string Thomas that was returned by the `DataLoader`. Instead it contains the value `undefined`.

```
let ac = new AdminController(new DataLoader());
ac.loadName();
console.log(ac.adminName); // Logs "undefined", not "Thomas"
```

Listing 8.14: 08\06_functionsAndThis\main.ts

That means the keyword `this` does not point to the `AdminController`-instance in the callback-function of the `loadName`-method:

```
loadName() {
    this.dataLoader.loadAdminName(function (loadedName) {
        this._adminName = loadedName;
    })
}
```

Listing 8.15: 08\06_functionsAndThis\main.ts

But hey, we are developers, we can program a solution for that problem. Listing 8.16 shows it: Before we use the `DataLoader`-instance in the `loadName`-method, we just store the value of `this` in a local variable called `_this`. Now we are sure that we have a reference to the `AdminController`-instance in that local variable. Inside of the callback-function we use our local variable `_this` to access the `_adminName`-field of our `AdminController`-instance.

```
loadName() {
    let _this = this;
    this.dataLoader.loadAdminName(function (loadedName) {
        _this._adminName = loadedName;
    })
}
```

Listing 8.16: 08\06_functionsAndThis\main.ts

With the adjusted `loadName`-method, the `AdminController` works as expected. In listing 8.17 the `adminName`-property is accessed after we called the `loadName`-method on the `AdminController`-instance. The `adminName`-property is not undefined anymore, now it contains the expected value Thomas.

```
let ac = new AdminController(new DataLoader());
ac.loadName();
console.log(ac.adminName); // Logs "Thomas"
```

Listing 8.17: 08\06_functionsAndThis\main.ts

Instead of using the workaround of listing 8.16, TypeScript and ES2015 have a better solution to the `this`-problem: Arrow functions.

Arrow Functions

In the previous section, we have created the `AdminController`-class shown in listing 8.18.

```
class AdminController {
    private _adminName: string;

    get adminName(): string { return this._adminName; }

    constructor(private dataLoader: DataLoader) { }

    loadName() {
        this.dataLoader.loadAdminName(function (loadedName) {
            this._adminName = loadedName;
        })
    }
}
```

Listing 8.18: 08\06_functionsAndThis\main.ts

We noticed that the `this`-keyword used in the callback function does not refer to the `AdminController`-instance, as the `this`-keyword is used in the context of the function.

TypeScript and ES2015 have a solution to this problem: Arrow functions. Listing 8.19 shows how the callback function in the `loadName`-method is written as an arrow function. The `loadedName`-parameter is defined in parentheses. After the parameter an arrow (=>) points to the function body.

```
loadName() {
    this.dataLoader.loadAdminName((loadedName) => {
        this._adminName = loadedName;
    })
}
```

Listing 8.19: 08\07_arrowFunctions\main.ts

The arrow function in listing 8.19 is not too much different from the classic function in listing 8.18, at least from a syntactical point of view. But when it comes to the `this`-keyword, the difference is huge. Arrow functions capture `this` lexically, which means the `this`-keyword refers to the outer context in which an arrow-function is executed in. That means the `this`-keyword in listing 8.19 points to the `AdminController`-instance, and that's exactly what we want.

With the arrow function in place, the `this`-keyword and so the code of listing 8.20 works as expected. After the `loadName`-method was called on the `AdminController`-instance in listing 8.20, the `adminName`-property is set as expected to the string Thomas.

```
let ac = new AdminController(new DataLoader());
ac.loadName();
console.log(ac.adminName); // Logs "Thomas"
```

Listing 8.20: 08\07_arrowFunctions\main.ts

Arrow functions are a native part of ES2015. But with TypeScript, you can compile them down to ES5 or even ES3. It gets really interesting when you look at the generated JavaScript code. Listing 8.21 shows the compiled ES5 code for the `loadName`-method of the `AdminController`-class that is using the arrow function. Somehow this looks familiar, doesn't it?

When compiling the arrow function to ES5, the TypeScript compiler uses exactly the same trick as we did. As you can see in listing 8.21, it stores this in a local _this-variable. Inside of the callback function it is using the local _this-variable to get a reference to the AdminController-instance to access its _adminName-property.

```
AdminController.prototype.loadName = function () {
    var _this = this;
    this.dataLoader.loadAdminName(function (loadedName) {
        _this._adminName = loadedName;
    });
};
```

Listing 8.21: main.js compiled as ES5

Listing 8.22 shows the loadName-method compiled to ES2015. As arrow functions are a native part of ES2015, the code looks exactly like our TypeScript code of listing 8.19.

```
loadName() {
    this.dataLoader.loadAdminName((loadedName) => {
        this._adminName = loadedName;
    });
}
```

Listing 8.22: main.js compiled as ES2015

> **Note**
>
> Due to the handling of this, you should always prefer arrow functions over classic functions.

Async and Await

To make asynchronous code easy to write, TypeScript supports the async and await keywords like known from languages like C#. Listing 8.23 shows a simple delay-function. It has a number-parameter that defines the number of milliseconds this method should delay.

```
function delay(ms: number) {
    return new Promise(resolve => setTimeout(resolve, ms));
}
```

Listing 8.23: 08\08_asyncAwait\main.ts

The `delay`-function of listing 8.23 returns a `Promise`-object. The `Promise`-object uses the `setTimeout`-function to resolve after the passed in milliseconds.

The `Promise`-class is new in ES2015 and is used for asynchronous calculations. When you have a `Promise`, you can use the `await`-keyword in TypeScript to wait for the `Promise` to return. The function in which you are using the `await`-keyword needs to be marked as asynchronous with the `async`-keyword.

Listing 8.24 shows an asynchronous `main`-function. It is awaiting the `delay`-function multiple times and logs to the browser's console in between. When the `main`-function is called, the single logs are written sequentially after each other to the browser's console, always with a gap of 1000 milliseconds.

```
async function main() {
    await delay(1000);
    console.log("This");

    await delay(1000);
    console.log("is ");

    await delay(1000);
    console.log("ASYNC!");
}
main();
```

Listing 8.24: 08\08_asyncAwait\main.ts

The keywords `async` and `await` are a native part of ES2017. When you compile the TypeScript code of listing 8.24 to ES2017, you'll see the output of listing 8.25. It looks exactly the same as the TypeScript code, just without the type annotations.

```
function delay(ms) {
    return new Promise(resolve => setTimeout(resolve, ms));
}
async function main() {
    await delay(1000);
    console.log("This");
    await delay(1000);
    console.log("is ");
    await delay(1000);
    console.log("ASYNC!");
}
main();
```

Listing 8.25: *ES2017 supports async and await natively*

> **Note**
>
> With TypeScript 2.1 you can compile async await down to ES5 or even ES3. But the `Promise`-class is not available there. You need to get a Promise polyfill. A polyfill is a JavaScript-library that brings a JavaScript-feature not available in the browser to your application by just referencing that JavaScript-library.

Summary

In this chapter, you learned about the types of functions available in JavaScript: Named and anonymous functions.

You learned about optional, default and rest parameters in TypeScript and how to pass a function as a parameter to another function. You've also seen how to define an interface for your function.

When you use functions inside of the methods of your classes, you should always use arrow functions instead of classic functions. With arrow functions the `this`-keyword points as expected to the instance of your class.

The last thing you learned in this chapter were asynchronous functions in TypeScript with the keywords `async` and `await`. They are a native part of ES2017.

9. Modules

Introduction

So far, we've written our TypeScript code into a single *.ts*-file. But when you build a larger application, you might want to structure and organize your code across different *.ts*-files, and not just in a single *.ts*-file. With modules, you can exactly do this. In addition, each file has its own scope when you use modules. You need to explicitly export things like classes or variables to be able to import them in other files.

Modules are a native part of ES2015 and also available in TypeScript. In TypeScript, you can compile modules even down to ES5 or ES3.

In this chapter, we look at the module basics where you read what a module is exactly. Then you learn how to export and import from a module and how to set up a module loader. You also learn how to export and import multiple types from a module and how to use aliases for exports and imports.

> Note: Namespaces
>
> Beside modules, TypeScript also supports a concept called "namespaces" to structure and organize your code. While namespaces are a TypeScript specific concept, modules are a native part of ES2015.
>
> That's the reason why it is recommended to use modules instead of namespaces for your new projects. In chapter 12, "Angular with TypeScript", you'll see that modules are heavily used when you build an application with Angular and TypeScript.

Module Basics

When you hear the term module you might think of a packaged item or something like a container. But it isn't as complicated. In fact, a module in TypeScript and so in ES2015 is very simple:

> A *.ts*-file in TypeScript is a module, if it has at least one import or one export at the root level of the file.

That's it. But is the advantage of using modules just splitting up your TypeScript code across multiple files?

No, there's more about just splitting the code across several files: Inside of a *.ts*-file, or let's say inside of a module, the code is executed within the scope of the module, and not within the global scope.

That means that functions, classes, variables and everything else that you create inside of your module are only visible to your module itself. If you want some parts to be visible to other modules, you have to explicitly export them. And even if you export for example a class from your module, another module has to explicitly import that class to be able to use it.

So, it's all about exporting and importing from modules. Time to get our hands dirty. Let's write some code.

Export and Import

Listing 9.1 shows the contents of the *friends.ts*-file. The file contains a `Friend`-class and a `Developer`-class that inherits from `Friend`. Note the `export`-keyword in front of the `Developer`-class. This makes the *friends.ts*-file a module, as it exports that `Developer`-class. Like mentioned in the previous section: Every *.ts*-file that has at least one import or export is a module, and as the *friends.ts*-file in listing 9.1 exports the `Developer`-class, it is a module. Other modules can import the exported `Developer`-class in order to use it. The `Friend`-class defined in listing 9.1 is not visible to other modules, as it is not exported.

```
class Friend {
    constructor(public firstName: string) { }
}
export class Developer extends Friend {
    knowsTypeScript: boolean;
}
```

Listing 9.1: 09\01_modules_SimpleExportImport\friends.ts

Listing 9.2 shows the *main.ts*-file. At the top, there's an import statement. The `Developer`-class is imported from the friends-module. With this import, the `Developer`-class can be used inside of the *main.ts*-file. And as the *main.ts*-file contains an import statement, it is also a module.

```
import { Developer } from './friends';

var dev = new Developer("Thomas");
dev.knowsTypeScript = true;
```

Listing 9.2: 09\01_modules_SimpleExportImport\main.ts

Now let's look at the import statement of listing 9.2. After the `import`-keyword you define the class that you want to import in curly braces. In listing 9.2 it's the `Developer`-class. Then you specify the module from which you want to import that class. You do this by using the `from`-keyword followed by the path to the module. In listing 9.2 the path is `./friends`. The dot takes the current folder where the *main.ts*-file respectively the generated *main.js*-file is in. Then it looks in that folder for the *friends.js*-file that was generated from the *friend.ts*-file. That *friends.js*-file contains the module. The file-extension for the module is optional, but you could be explicit and add a *.js*-extension if you want to:

```
import { Developer } from './friends.js';
```

The *.js*-extension is optional, and normally, you never add that extension explicitly. The statement above is just to show you that the import statement actually refers to the *friends.js*-file. When you omit the *.js*-extension, your module loader will add it for you.

But wait, module loader, we never talked about it, right?

Setting Up a Module Loader

Modules are a native part of TypeScript and ES2015. But today's browsers are not able to load modules on their own. You need to set up a module loader that is able to load modules. A module loader walks down all the dependencies from your root-module. Based on the import statements that you wrote in TypeScript a module loader finds all the required *.js*-files and loads them accordingly.

In the previous section, we've created the files *main.js* and *friends.js*. In *main.js* we have an import for *friends.js*. We can give the *main.js*-file to a module loader, and it will find out that it has to load the *friends.js*-file in addition, because it finds the import statement in the *main.js*-file.

There are several formats for modules around. Depending on which module loader you're using, you need to set the `module-compiler` option in your *tsconfig.json*-file accordingly. You could set it for example to `es2015` like in listing 9.3 if that format is supported by the module loader you're using.

```
{
    "compilerOptions": {
        "module": "es2015",
        "target": "es5",
        "noImplicitAny": false,
        "sourceMap": false
    }
}
```

Listing 9.3: tsconfig.json with module-format set to es2015

With the module-format es2015, the generated *main.js*-file contains exactly the same import-syntax as we've written in the *main.ts*-file in listing 9.2:

```
import { Developer } from './friends';
var dev = new Developer("Thomas");
dev.knowsTypeScript = true;
```

Listing 9.4: main.js with es2015 module format

That means the import/export syntax of TypeScript is matching the ES2015 syntax. As TypeScript is a superset of JavaScript, this is nothing to wonder about, it's consequential that TypeScript is using the ES2015 syntax.

Instead of es2015, you can set the `module-compiler` option in the *tsconfig.json*-file also to one of these values:

- none
- commonjs
- system
- amd
- umd

In this chapter, we'll use the commonjs-format. Commonjs is a module format that is supported natively by Node.js. When you specify commonjs for the `module`-compiler option in the *tsconfig.json*-file, the generated *main.js*-file contains the `require`-syntax (listing 9.5) to import the friends-module.

```
"use strict";
var friends_1 = require("./friends");
var dev = new friends_1.Developer("Thomas");
dev.knowsTypeScript = true;
```

Listing 9.5: *main.js with commonjs module format*

The commonjs-format is the default format specified when you create a new *tsconfig.json*-file by calling the following command:

```
tsc --init
```

The *tsconfig.json*-file that we use in this chapter is shown in listing 9.6. It has the commonjs-format specified.

```
{
    "compilerOptions": {
        "module": "commonjs",
        "target": "es5",
        "noImplicitAny": false,
        "sourceMap": false
    }
}
```

Listing 9.6: *09\01_modules_SimpleExportImport\tsconfig.json*

Now we need to set up a module loader. We'll use SystemJS, a common and popular module loader. SystemJS supports several module formats, including the commonjs-format that we've specified in the *tsconfig.json*-file in listing 9.6.

The first thing we need to do is to create a *package.json*-file. We need this, so that we can add SystemJS as a dependency to our project. To create a *package.json*-file you can use the Node Package Manager (npm). We have used npm already in chapter 2, "Setting up Your Environment", to install TypeScript.

Just go to the command line and run this command on the root-folder of your project to create a *package.json*-file:

```
npm init
```

The `npm init` command is asking you for input on the command line. It uses the input to create a *package.json*-file. You can enter a name, a version, a description and much more for your package. For our little sample used here, you can just enter a name, then press Enter multiple times, then type in yourself as an author and press again Enter until the *package.json*-file is created. Below you see how the command line looked on my machine after I called the `npm init` command. I just entered the name `typescript-book-module-sample1` and myself as an author, everything else is blank, because I just hit enter without specifying a value:

```
name: (02_modules_SimpleExportImport) typescript-book-module-sample1
version: (1.0.0)
description:
entry point: (main.js)
test command:
git repository:
keywords:
author: Thomas Claudius Huber
license: (ISC)
```

After the information has been entered by using the `npm init` command, the *package.json*-file is generated like shown in listing 9.7.

```
{
  "name": "typescript-book-module-sample1",
  "version": "1.0.0",
  "description": "",
  "main": "main.js",
  "scripts": {
    "test": "echo \"Error: no test specified\" && exit 1"
  },
  "author": "Thomas Claudius Huber",
  "license": "ISC"
}
```

Listing 9.7: Generated package.json-file

> **Note**
>
> If you don't want to specify anything for your *package.json*-file on the command line, you can run the `npm init` command with the `-y` parameter:
>
> `npm init -y`
>
> The output will be similar to listing 9.7, just with an empty author and with the name of your folder as package name.

Now let's install SystemJS. Just go back to the command line and enter this command to install SystemJS:

```
npm install systemjs --save
```

Note the `--save` parameter in the command above. This tells npm to store the systemjs dependency in the *package.json*-file. So, after running that command, you see a new entry in your *package.json*-file like shown in listing 9.8.

```
"dependencies": {
  "systemjs": "^0.19.41"
}
```

Listing 9.8: 09\01_modules_SimpleExportImport\package.json

The `npm install` command will create a *node_modules*-folder in your project-folder. This *node_modules*-folder contains all the dependencies your project requires to run. By installing SystemJS, you find for example a folder called *systemjs* that is in the *node_modules*-folder.

To be able to use SystemJS in our app, the *index.html*-file needs to be loaded via http, and not directly opened from the file-system. That means we need a small webserver that is able to serve the *index.html*-file to the browser via http. The lite-server is a light-weight web server that is ideal to use for this scenario. And of course, it is also available as a package in npm. To install it, run this command:

```
npm install lite-server --save-dev
```

Beside the lite-server we also install the concurrently-library. That's a library that allows you to run two or more commands concurrently. To install it from npm, run this command.

```
npm install concurrently --save-dev
```

You may have noticed that we have installed the packages lite-server and concurrently by using the --save-dev parameter. That parameter adds the installed packages as developer dependencies to your *package.json*-file like shown in listing 9.9. These devDependencies are only required for development, but they're not required to deploy your application.

```
"devDependencies": {
  "concurrently": "^3.1.0",
  "lite-server": "^2.2.2"
}
```

Listing 9.9: 09\01_modules_SimpleExportImport\package.json

With the packages concurrently and lite-server installed, you can add a script called start to the *package.json*-file. Just put it like in listing 9.10 under a scripts-property. As you can see, the script in listing 9.10 runs the typescript compiler with tsc. Then it uses the installed concurrently-library to start up the TypeScript Compiler in watch-mode with tsc -w and to fire up the lite-server.

```
"scripts": {
  "start": "tsc && concurrently \"tsc -w\" \"lite-server\" "
},
```

Listing 9.10: 09\01_modules_SimpleExportImport\package.json

With the start-script defined in the *package.json*-file, you can go to the command line and execute the script by entering this command:

```
npm start
```

But the application doesn't work yet, as we haven't set up SystemJS. But we're done with the required dependencies and with the start-script. So, our *package.json*-file is complete. Listing 9.11 shows the whole file.

```json
{
  "name": "typescript-book-module-sample1",
  "version": "1.0.0",
  "description": "",
  "main": "main.js",
  "scripts": {
    "start": "tsc && concurrently \"tsc -w\" \"lite-server\" "
  },
  "author": "Thomas Claudius Huber",
  "license": "ISC",
  "dependencies": {
    "systemjs": "^0.19.41"
  },
  "devDependencies": {
    "concurrently": "^3.1.0",
    "lite-server": "^2.2.2"
  }
}
```

Listing 9.11: 09\01_modules_SimpleExportImport\package.json

To use SystemJS, we need to include the code of that library in our *index.html*-file. Listing 9.12 shows how the *system.js*-file is referenced in a `script`-tag that is placed inside of the `head`-element of the *index.html*-file.

```
<head>
  <title>Getting started with TypeScript</title>
  <script src="node_modules/systemjs/dist/system.js"></script>
</head>
```

Listing 9.12: 09\01_modules_SimpleExportImport\index.html

Now let's use SystemJS in the body of the *index.html*-file to load our root module contained in the *main.js*-file.

Listing 9.13 shows the setup in the body-element. Inside of a script-element the config-function of SystemJS is called. The baseURL tells SystemJS what's the root path where it should start to look for modules. The defaultJSExtensions-option is set to true. This allows us to omit the *.js*-extension when we reference other modules in an import statement. After the configuration, the System.import-function is called. It loads the *main.js*-module from the current folder that is referenced with a dot. Note that the optional *.js*-extension is already omitted, it's just main and not main.js. After the import-call there's a success callback-function and an error-callback function, both just log to the console. That's it, SystemJS is set up and the main-module is loaded.

```
<body>
  <script>
        SystemJS.config({
            baseURL:'/',
            defaultJSExtensions: true
        });
        System.import('./main')
            .then(function(){console.log('loaded');})
            .catch(function(err){ console.error(err); });
  </script>
     <p>Look in the browser's console</p>
</body>
```

Listing 9.13: 09\01_modules_SimpleExportImport\index.html

Now we're ready to go. Just go to the command line and run the start-script defined in the *package.json*-file by executing this command:

```
npm start
```

This automatically fires up a browser with the application. SystemJS loads the module from *main.js*, and due to the import statement in that module it also loads the module from *friends.js*.

The lite-server is started and it supports a feature called browser sync. When you change your TypeScript code, it gets compiled as the TypeScript compiler is started in watch mode. Lite-server will also automatically refresh the browser with the latest compiled JavaScript.

To stop the server, press Ctrl+C on the command line.

Now we're done, congrats. You've successfully set up SystemJS and you've defined two modules in TypeScript with import and export statements.

How to Install Dependencies for a Project

When you download projects from the web, like the samples of this book, you might find a *package.json*-file in those projects. If that's the case, you need to install the dependencies defined in that *package.json*-file. Just open a console and run this command:

```
npm install
```

The `npm install` command will look into the *package.json*-file of the current folder. Then it downloads all the dependencies and devDependencies defined in that file into a local *node_modules*-folder.

For the samples of this book, the *package.json*-file also contains a start-script. So, after you've installed all the dependencies with `npm install` you can start the application with this command:

```
npm start
```

Export Multiple Types

So far, we've just exported the `Developer`-class from the friends-module. Listing 9.14 contains an additional class called `Skateboarder` that is exported as well.

```
class Friend {
    constructor(public firstName: string) { }
}
export class Developer extends Friend {
    knowsTypeScript: boolean;
}
export class Skateboarder extends Friend {
    makeKickflip() {
        console.log(this.firstName + " made a kickflip");
    }
}
```

Listing 9.14: 09\02_modules_MultipleExportImport\friends.ts

Instead of writing the `export`-keyword in front of the class, you can also export all the classes with a single export statement like in listing 9.15.

```
class Friend {
    constructor(public firstName: string) { }
}
class Developer extends Friend {
    knowsTypeScript: boolean;
}
class Skateboarder extends Friend {
    makeKickflip() {
        console.log(this.firstName + " made a kickflip");
    }
}
export { Developer, Skateboarder }
```

Listing 9.15: *Export two classes in a single statement*

Import Multiple Types

When you import multiple types from a module, you just separate them with a comma. Listing 9.16 shows the *main.ts*-file that is importing the classes `Developer` and `Skateboarder` from the friends-module.

```
import { Developer, Skateboarder } from './friends';

var dev = new Developer("Julia");
dev.knowsTypeScript = true;

var boarder = new Skateboarder("Thomas");
boarder.makeKickflip();
```

Listing 9.16: *09\02_modules_MultipleExportImport\main.ts*

Instead of importing every single item from a module, you can also import the whole module with a star. Then you have to specify an alias for the module with the `as`-keyword. Listing 9.17 shows how the friends-module is imported with the alias `Friends`. To access for example the `Developer`-class in your code, you have to use that `Friends`-alias in front of the class name like this: `Friends.Developer`.

```
import * as Friends from './friends';

var dev = new Friends.Developer("Julia");
dev.knowsTypeScript = true;


var boarder = new Friends.Skateboarder("Thomas");
boarder.makeKickflip();
```
Listing 9.17: 09\03_modules_ImportWholeModule\main.ts

Use Export Aliases

When you export an item, you can give it an alias. Then the other modules are not able to see your internal names, but just the alias. Listing 9.18 exports the `Developer`-class under the alias `Coder`.

```
class Friend {
    constructor(public firstName: string) { }
}
class Developer extends Friend {
    knowsTypeScript: boolean;
}
export { Developer as Coder }
```
Listing 9.18: 09\04_modules_ExportAlias\friends.ts

When the module is imported in another module, that alias is used. Listing 9.19 imports the `Coder`. Note also how the class is used. The name of the `Developer`-class is not visible in the module of listing 9.19, just its alias.

```
import { Coder } from './friends';

var dev = new Coder("Thomas");
dev.knowsTypeScript = true;
```
Listing 9.19: 09\04_modules_ExportAlias\main.ts

Use Import Aliases

Like for exports, you can also use aliases on imports. The friends-module in listing 9.20 exports the `Developer`-class.

```
class Friend {
    constructor(public firstName: string) { }
}
export class Developer extends Friend {
    knowsTypeScript: boolean;
}
```

Listing 9.20: 09\05_modules_ImportAlias\friends.ts

The main-module in listing 9.21 imports the `Developer`-class from listing 9.20. But on the import, it is specifying the alias `Programmer`. That means inside of this module, the alias `Programmer` is used to create new developers.

```
import { Developer as Programmer } from './friends';

var prog = new Programmer("Thomas");
prog.knowsTypeScript = true;
```

Listing 9.21: 09\05_modules_ImportAlias\main.ts

Creating an import alias is especially useful when you import classes from different modules that have the same name. Then an import-alias allows you to differentiate between the imported classes.

Default Export

Sometimes you have just a single export in your module that is important. Then you can use the `default`-keyword to mark that export as the default. Listing 9.22 marks the `Developer`-class as a default export.

```
export class Friend {
    constructor(public firstName: string) { }
}
export default class Developer extends Friend {
    knowsTypeScript: boolean;
}
```

Listing 9.22: 09\06_modules_defaultExports\friends.ts

> **Note**
> You can specify only one default-export per module.

When you import a default-export, you don't need the curly braces. You also don't have to use the name of the default export, you can specify any name you want. Listing 9.23 imports the default-export of the friends-module – which is the `Developer`-class from listing 9.22. It specifies the name Coder under which that default export is used in this file.

```
import Coder from './friends';

var prog = new Coder("Thomas");
prog.knowsTypeScript = true;
```
Listing 9.23: 09\06_modules_defaultExports\main.ts

But now the question is: How do you import the other exports in addition? When you look at listing 9.22, you can see that the `Friend`-class is also exported. To import the `Friend`-class in addition to the default export, you just specify it after the default export in curly braces. Listing 9.24 shows the required import statement.

```
import Coder, { Friend } from './friends';
var prog = new Coder("Thomas");
prog.knowsTypeScript = true;

var friend = new Friend("Julia");
console.log(friend.firstName);
```
Listing 9.24: 09\06_modules_defaultExports\main.ts

Exporting Variables and Functions

You cannot export just classes and interfaces from your module, you can also export variables and functions. Listing 9.25 shows a friends-module that exports the `FRIENDS`-variable that contains an array of friends. It also exports the function `printFriend`.

```
class Friend {
    constructor(public firstName: string) { }
}
export let FRIENDS: Friend[] = [
    new Friend("Sara"),
    new Friend("Anna"),
    new Friend("Thomas")];

export function printFriend(friend:Friend){
    console.log(friend.firstName);
}
```
Listing 9.25: 09\07_modules_variablesAndFunctions\friends.ts

As shown with classes, you could also export these two items in a single export statement like shown in listing 9.26.

```
class Friend {
    constructor(public firstName: string) { }
}
let FRIENDS: Friend[] = [
    new Friend("Sara"),
    new Friend("Anna"),
    new Friend("Thomas")];

function printFriend(friend: Friend) {
    console.log(friend.firstName);
}
export { FRIENDS, printFriend }
```
Listing 9.26: Export the variable and the function in one statement

Listing 9.27 shows the main-module that is importing the two items from listing 9.25/9.26. It iterates over the array stored in the FRIENDS-variable and calls the imported printFriend-function for each Friend-instance.

```
import { FRIENDS, printFriend } from './friends';

for (let friend of FRIENDS) {
    printFriend(friend);
}
```
Listing 9.27: 09\07_modules_variablesAndFunctions\main.ts

> **Note**
> The `Friend`-class is not necessary for the code of listing 9.27. We're just getting an existing array with `Friend`-instances that we pass to the `printFriend`-function. But as we don't have the `Friend`-class in the *main.ts*-file, we cannot call the constructor with `new Friend` in that file.

Summary

In this chapter, you learned to organize your code in separate files by using modules. Modules are a native part of ES2015 and so also available in TypeScript.

A module is a *.ts*-file that has at least one import or one export.

Modules have their own scope. The functions, variables, interfaces and classes that you create inside of a module are only visible to the module itself, unless you explicitly export them. Other modules still need to explicitly import your exported items to be able to use them.

Modules are not supported in today's browsers. To be able to use modules, you need to set up a module loader. In this chapter, you learned how to set up SystemJS to load your modules.

Beside simple exports and imports, you've also seen in this chapter how to create aliases and how to use default exports.

In chapter 12, "Angular with TypeScript", you'll see that you're using modules intensively when you build an Angular-application with TypeScript.

Now let's continue with Decorators in TypeScript.

10. Decorators

Introduction

TypeScript supports decorators to annotate classes and its members. Decorators in TypeScript are similar to attributes in C# or annotations in Java.

Decorators are in a proposal state for JavaScript, which means they will be part of a future ECMAScript standard. But the proposal for decorators is not finalized. Anyway, in TypeScript decorators are available as an experimental feature. "Experimental" as the proposal for JavaScript might still change before it gets into the standard.

Popular frameworks like Angular make heavy use of decorators in TypeScript. You'll see this in action in chapter 12, "Angular with TypeScript".

In this chapter, you learn the basics about decorators. You learn how to create a simple property decorator that logs changes to the console. You also read how to create a class decorator that stores meta-information for that class by using the reflect-metadata library.

> **Note**
> Aim of this chapter is that you understand how decorators work. This knowledge pays out for you when you learn a framework like Angular that makes use of decorators.

Decorator Basics

The following snippet shows the decorator `Component` on the `Friend`-class:

```
@Component
class Friend{ }
```

As you can see, a decorator starts with an @-character. The decorator itself must be an expression that evaluates to a function that has a specific signature. The required signature depends on where the decorator is used. For example, a class decorator needs to evaluate to a function that has a single parameter of type `Function`.

Listing 10.1 shows such a class decorator. The function `Component` matches the required signature for a class decorator, hence it can be used on the `Friend`-class with a leading @-character.

```
function Component(target: Function){
}

@Component
class Friend{
}
```

Listing 10.1: A simple class decorator

TypeScript decorators can be set on different targets :
- class
- property
- accessor
- method
- parameter

In this chapter, we'll create a property and class decorator.

Turn on Decorator Support

Before you can start with decorators, you should open up your *tsconfig.json*-file. Set the compiler option for experimental decorators like in listing 10.2 to true.

```
{
    "compilerOptions": {
        "module": "commonjs",
        "target": "es5",
        "noImplicitAny": false,
        "sourceMap": false,
        "experimentalDecorators": true
    }
}
```

Listing 10.2: tsconfig.json with experimental decorators option set to true

Create a Property Decorator

To find out the signature for a property decorator, you have different options, here are two:

Option 1: Go to the official docs on http://www.typescriptlang.org.

Option 2: As you're a developer, you might care more about the code than about the documentation. So, you should go to the TypeScript repository on https://github.com/Microsoft/TypeScript. Search in that repository for PropertyDecorator. You'll find this signature that is required to build a property decorator:

```
declare type PropertyDecorator = (target: Object, propertyKey: string
 | symbol) => void;
```

Now you know the signature: A property decorator needs to have two parameters, the target-object and the property key, and it returns void. With that knowledge, you can build your own decorator. Let's assume you want to build a property decorator that logs every access to the decorated property to the console, and you want to call the decorator logAccess.

Let's start with an empty logAccess-function like in listing 10.3 that has the correct signature for a property decorator. The decorator is used on the name-property of the Friend-class.

```
function logAccess(target: Object,propertyKey: string){
}

class Friend {
    @logAccess
    name:string;
}
```

Listing 10.3: A simple logChanges decorator

The idea is now to replace the original name-property in the Friend-class with a brand-new property, so that we can log the access to the property in the setter and in the getter. And this replacement should happen in the decorator.

Listing 10.4 shows the implemented `logAccess`-function. First the value is grabbed for the property and stored in the `value`-variable. Then a function for the setter and a function for the getter is defined. Note how both functions log the property key and the value to the console.

At the end the original property is replaced in two steps: First the original property is deleted from the object. If that was successful, a new property is defined in a second step by calling the `Object.defineProperty`-method. As a first argument, the target-object is passed to that method, then the property key, and then an object that defines the get and set functions. Here the `getter` and `setter` functions are used that we've created before.

```typescript
function logAccess(target: Object, propertyKey: string) {
    // grab the value
    let value = this[propertyKey];

    // define a setter
    let setter = (newValue) => {
        value = newValue;
        console.log(`set ${propertyKey}: ${value}`);
    };

    // define a getter
    let getter = () => {
        console.log(`get ${propertyKey}: ${value}`);
        return value;
    };

    // replace the property
    if (delete this[propertyKey]) {
        Object.defineProperty(
            target, propertyKey, {
                get: getter,
                set: setter
            });
    }
}
```

Listing 10.4: *10\01_propertyDecorator\main.ts*

With the code of listing 10.4, our little `logAccess` property decorator is ready for a test. In listing 10.5 the `logAccess` property decorator is set on the `name`-property of the `Friend`-class.

```
class Friend {
    @logAccess
    name: string;
}

let friend = new Friend();
friend.name = "Thomas";
friend.name = "Julia";
let firstName = friend.name;
```

Listing 10.5: 10\01_propertyDecorator\main.ts

As you can see in listing 10.5, a `Friend`-instance is created. Then the `name`-property is set to Thomas, then to Julia and then the `name`-property is read and the value is stored in the `firstName`-variable. When you look into the browser's console, you'll see this output created by the logic defined in our awesome `logAccess` property decorator:

```
set name: Thomas
set name: Julia
get name: Julia
```

Create a Class Decorator

Listing 10.6 shows a simple class decorator called `Component` like we've seen it at the beginning of this chapter. As you can see, `Component` is just a function that has a single parameter of type `Function`. This is the signature like it is required for a class decorator.

```
function Component(target: Function){
}

@Component
class Friend{
}
```

Listing 10.6: A simple class decorator

Now let's assume you want to store the firstname and lastname of the class-author via that `Component`-decorator. You need two additional parameters. But wait, what about the required signature?

Of course, we need to match the signature for a class decorator, so we cannot add just two parameters. But there's a solution:

A decorator function itself does not need to match the required signature, but it needs to be an expression that evaluates to a function that has the required signature. This sounds a bit complicated, but it's quite simple: Just create a function that returns a function that has the required signature. Then the outer function can have any parameters you want. This approach is also called a decorator factory.

Listing 10.7 shows the Component-function that is such a decorator factory. The function itself has the parameters firstName and lastName. It returns a function that matches the required signature for a class decorator.

```
function Component(firstName: string, lastName: string) {
    return function MyDecorator(target: Function) {
    }
}
```

Listing 10.7: A decorator factory

On a class, you can use the decorator factory of listing 10.7 like this:

```
@Component("Thomas","Huber")
class Friend {
}
```

Instead of using a lot of parameters on the Component-function you could also define your own data object with an interface like in listing 10.8.

```
interface ComponentData {
    firstName: string;
    lastName: string;
}

function Component(data: ComponentData) {
    return function Component(target: Function) {
    }
}
```

Listing 10.8: 10\02_classDecorator\main.ts

With the ComponentData-interface of listing 10.8, the usage of the Component-Decorator looks like in listing 10.9. Very readable.

```
@Component({
    firstName: "Thomas",
    lastName: "Huber"
})
class Friend {
}
```

Listing 10.9: 10\02_classDecorator\main.ts

Now we have that Component-decorator. But we don't store the received data anywhere. Inside of the decorator function we should do this:

```
function Component(data: ComponentData) {
    return function Component(target: Function) {
        // TODO: Store the data somehere
    }
}
```

To store the data, you could use your custom logic, or you could use the reflect-metadata library that is part of the decorator proposal for JavaScript.

Use the Reflect-metadata Library

To use the reflect-metadata library, you need to install it from npm by calling this command in a console window:

```
npm install reflect-metadata
```

And if you want to save it to your *package.json*-file, add the --save parameter in addition.

```
npm install reflect-metadata --save
```

In the samples of this book you find a project in the folder *10\02_classDecorator* that has everything set up in its *package.json*-file. Beside the reflect-metadata library it contains dependencies for lite-server and for the module loader SystemJS that you know already from chapter 9, "Modules". So, just go to that folder, open a command line and run this:

```
npm install
```

Now you can focus on the Component-decorator again. Listing 10.10 shows how the reflect-metadata module is imported. With the defineMetadata-function the ComponentData is stored for the target-object under a componentDataKey that we've specified as a simple string.

```
import 'reflect-metadata';

interface ComponentData {
    firstName: string;
    lastName: string;
}
let componentDataKey = "componentData";

function Component(data: ComponentData) {
    return function Component(target: Function) {
        Reflect.defineMetadata(componentDataKey, data, target);
    }
}
```

Listing 10.10: 10\02_classDecorator\main.ts

> **Note**
> That import statement in listing 10.10 is interesting, right? We haven't seen this in chapter 9, "Modules". This import statement loads the module reflect-metadata without any imports. The module reflect-metadata adds the Reflect-object to the global namespace, so it's available in listing 10.10.

On the Friend-class the Component-decorator is used with a firstName and lastName like specified in listing 10.11.

```
@Component({
    firstName: "Thomas",
    lastName: "Huber"
})
class Friend {
}
```

Listing 10.11: 10\02_classDecorator\main.ts

As the data is stored for the Friend-class via the reflect-metadata library, we can use that library now to read that metadata. Listing 10.12 shows how the getMetadata-function is called with the componentDataKey and the Friend-class to get the defined ComponentData-object. The values of the properties firstName and lastName are logged to the console.

```
let compData = Reflect.getMetadata(componentDataKey, Friend)
                as ComponentData;
console.log(compData.firstName); // Logs "Thomas"
console.log(compData.lastName);  // Logs "Huber"
```

Listing 10.12: 10\02_classDecorator\main.ts

Now our class decorator is complete. It stores the defined values and you can read them again when you need them.

Component Decorator in Angular

When you build applications with Angular, you'll come across many different decorators. Listing 10.13 shows a simple angular component. The class `AppComponent` has a class decorator called `Component`. The `Component`-decorator is imported from the `@angular/core`-module. The decorator takes an object that defines a `selector` and a `template`. The `selector` is the html-tag that is used to reference this component. The `template` defines the UI of the component. It's a simple html-snippet that can contain Angular-magic.

```
import { Component } from '@angular/core';

@Component({
  selector: 'my-app',
  template: `<h1>Hello {{name}}</h1>`
})
export class AppComponent {
  name:string="Thomas";
}
```

Listing 10.13: A simple Angular component.

As you can see in the template in listing 10.13, Angular allows you to bind to properties of your decorated class. In Listing 10.13 the name-property is bound in html. By defining the UI via a decorator and by connecting it to the class with data binding, angular has a clear separation between UI and UI-logic. If you're familiar with patterns like Model-View-ViewModel (MVVM), this might look familiar to you, as it is a similar approach.

In chapter 12, "Angular with TypeScript", you learn more about Angular and its powerful data binding engine. The idea of this section was just to show you how a decorator is used in the Angular framework.

Summary

TypeScript allows you to annotate classes, properties, accessors, methods and parameters with decorators. Depending on where you use your decorator, it must have a specific signature.

When you want to pass data to a decorator, you need to create a decorator factory. A decorator factory is a function that can have any parameters you like. But the function itself returns a function that matches the signature required by the decorator.

Note that decorators might change in the future, as they're still in a proposal state for a future JavaScript standard. TypeScript allows you to use them in an experimental state.

11. Declaration Files

Introduction

When you use JavaScript libraries in your project, you might want to have the types available when you program with TypeScript. Else you don't get all the great features like compile-time errors and tooling. To get the types, you need to add type declarations to your project. This is what we look at in this chapter.

We start by including a simple JavaScript library in a small project. You learn how to create declarations for that library.

Then you'll learn about the lodash-library that we install from npm. You'll learn how to install the type declarations for this and other libraries via npm.

In the last section of this chapter, you read how you can create your own libraries with type declarations by using a TypeScript compiler option.

Include a Simple JavaScript-library

Let's assume you've written a small JavaScript-library in a file called *myLibrary.js* that contains just that simple `printFirstName`-function of listing 11.1. The `printFirstName`-function writes the `firstName`-property of the passed in `friend`-object to the html-document. Note that there are no types involved, as this is pure JavaScript.

```
function printFirstName(friend) {
    document.write("Firstname is " + friend.firstName);
}
```

Listing 11.1: 11\01_UseJsLibrary\myLibrary.js

To use the library in your project, you have to include it in the *index.html*-file via a script-tag like shown in listing 11.2.

```html
<!DOCTYPE html>
<html>
  <head>
    <title>Getting started with TypeScript</title>
    <script src="myLibrary.js"></script>
  </head>
  <body>
    <script src="main.js"></script>
    <p>Look in the browser's console</p>
  </body>
</html>
```

Listing 11.2: 11\01_UseJsLibrary\index.html

Now in your *main.ts*-file you could create a new object with a `firstName`-property and pass it to the `printFirstName`-function:

```
let friend = { firstName: "Thomas" };
printFirstName(friend);
```

Listing 11.3: 11\01_UseJsLibrary\main.ts

The code of listing 11.3 works, but there are no types involved. TypeScript even cannot find the `printFirstName`-function, as it does not know about the *myLibrary.js*-file, so you get an error like in figure 11.1. But TypeScript creates the JavaScript code anyway, and as the `printFirstName`-function exists at runtime, the code works as expected.

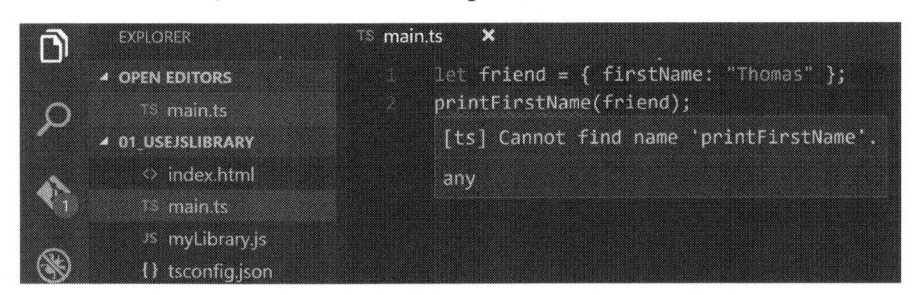

Figure 11.1: Visual Studio Code shows an error, printFirstName not found

To get rid of the error and to get static typing that supports you to pass in a correct parameter to the `printFirstName`-function, you can declare the `printFirstName`-function including an interface for its parameter.

Declare a Function

Listing 11.4 shows a declaration of the function `printFirstName`. Note how an interface is used to annotate the `friend`-parameter with that type. Also, note the `declare`-keyword. We declare the `printFirstName`-function, but there's no implementation in TypeScript. It's just a declaration to tell the TypeScript compiler "this is how the function looks like".

```
interface Friend {
    firstName: string;
}
declare function printFirstName(friend: Friend): void;

let friend = { firstName: "Thomas" };
printFirstName(friend);
```

Listing 11.4: 11\01_UseJsLibrary\main.ts

With the function declaration of listing 11.4, TypeScript knows the function. You don't get an error anymore when you use it. And with the `Friend`-interface in place, you get an error if you pass in an object to the `printFirstName`-function that does not have a `firstName`-property like defined by that `Friend`-interface.

Install Declaration Files from NPM

When you use libraries from npm, you might notice that you don't have any types available as well. Let's assume you're working on a project and you add the great lodash-library as a dependency to your project:

```
npm install lodash --save
```

Now you can use the library in your project. Listing 11.5 shows the *main.ts*-file that imports the `range`-function from the lodash-library.

```
import { range } from 'lodash';

let chapters = range(1, 12);
for (let num in chapters) {
    console.log(num);
}
```

Listing 11.5: 11\02_UseLodash\main.ts

The range-function is used in listing 11.5 to return an array with the numbers 1 to 12. Then this array is iterated in a for-loop. Every number is logged to the console.

When you write the range-function in listing 11.5, you don't get statement completion in Visual Studio Code. You don't see any information about the parameters of that function. Also, TypeScript and so Visual Studio Code does not know that the return type is a number-array. Instead TypeScript assumes the any type, as you can see in the tooltip in figure 11.2.

Figure 11.2: Without type declarations the range-function returns the type any

To get the type declarations for the lodash-library, you use the @types-organization available in npm. Just add a slash with your library-name and install the type declarations. For lodash it looks like this:

```
npm install @types/lodash --save-dev
```

With the `--save-dev` parameter the type declarations are saved as dev-dependencies in the *package.json*-file.

The installed type declarations are located in the file *node_modules/@types/lodash/index.d.ts*. Such a *.d.ts*-file is called a declaration file, as it contains just declarations.

With the type declarations installed, you can see in figure 11.3 that TypeScript and so Visual Studio Code knows now that the range-function returns a number-array.

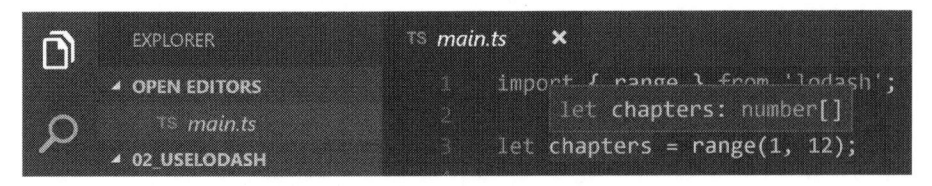

Figure 11.3: With type declarations, the range-function returns a number-array

When you use the lodash-library with the type declarations installed, you even get statement completion. Figure 11.4 shows the information that is displayed by Visual Studio Code for the range-function.

```
TS main.ts
1   import { range } from 'lodash';
2
3   let chapters = range(1,12)
4                          range(start: number, end: number, step?: number):
5   for (let num in (      number[]
6       console.log(r
7   }                      The start of the range.
                           Creates an array of numbers (positive and/or negative) progressing
                           from start up to, but not including, end. If end is not specified it's set
                           to start with start then set to 0. If end is less than start a zero-length
                       1/2 range is created unless a negative step is specified.
```

Figure 11.4: Statement completion with type declarations

You can also right-click the range-function and select "Go to definition" from the context menu. This will bring you to the declaration of the range-function in the file *node_modules/@types/lodash/index.d.ts*.

> **Note**
>
> If you want to know if type declarations are available for your favorite library, you can use Microsoft's type search that is located here:
> http://microsoft.github.io/TypeSearch/
>
> You can also look directly into the @types organization on the npm website:
> https://www.npmjs.com/~types
>
> The @types-organization is filled automatically with packages loaded from this GitHub repository:
> https://github.com/DefinitelyTyped/DefinitelyTyped

Write Your Own Library with Declarations

When you write your own library in TypeScript, you might want to push out declarations for the generated JavaScript code. Especially if you plan to publish your library via npm.

The great thing is: When you write your library in TypeScript, you get the type declarations for free, as there's a little compiler option to generate them.

Let's assume you've written the great library shown in listing 11.6. The `printFirstName`-function takes a `Friend`-object and writes its `firstName` to the html document.

```
interface Friend {
    firstName: string;
}

function printFirstName(friend: Friend) {
  document.write(friend.firstName);
}
```

Listing 11.6: *11\03_WriteALibrary\main.ts*

To generate declaration files for your library, open up the *tsconfig.json*-file and set the declaration compiler option like in listing 11.7 to `true`.

```
{
    "compilerOptions": {
        "module": "commonjs",
        "target": "es5",
        "noImplicitAny": false,
        "sourceMap": false,
        "declaration": true
    }
}
```

Listing 11.7: *11\03_WriteALibrary\tsconfig.json*

With the declaration compiler option set, the TypeScript compiler will not only create a *main.js*-file from your *main.ts*-file. It will also create a declaration file called *main.d.ts*. The d in the filename stands for declarations. Listing 11.8 shows the content of this declaration file for our little library. It contains the `Friend`-interface and a declaration for the `printFirstName`-function.

```
interface Friend {
    firstName: string;
}
declare function printFirstName(friend: Friend): void;
```

Listing 11.8: *11\03_WriteALibrary\main.d.ts*

> **Note**
> Files that contain type declarations usually always end with *d.ts*, it's a common convention. We call them declaration files.

Now you've written your library and you've generated the declaration file *main.d.ts*. But the question is: How do you publish your generated *main.js*-file together with the *main.d.ts*-file to npm?

You have two options:
1. You publish your *main.d.ts*-file bundled with your npm package
2. You publish your *main.d.ts*-file to the @types-organization to get the same behaviour as with the lodash-library in the previous section.

For the first option, you specify the *main.d.ts*-file in your *package.json*-file like in listing 11.9.

```
{
  "name": "my-awesome-library",
  "version": "1.0.0",
  "description": "",
  "main": "main.js",
  "types":"main.d.ts"
  ...
}
```

Listing 11.9: 11\03_WriteALibrary\package.json

For the second option – publishing to the @types-organization – you need to submit a pull request to this GitHub repository: https://github.com/DefinitelyTyped/DefinitelyTyped. The content of this repository is automatically published to the @types-organization in npm.

Summary

When you use an existing JavaScript-library, TypeScript does not know about the types, as JavaScript has no types. Without types, you don't get compile-time errors, you don't get the great tooling support with statement completion, go to definition and much more.

That's why TypeScript supports declaration files for existing JavaScript libraries. A declaration file is a normal TypeScript file that usually ends with *d.ts* and contains type declarations.

For all the popular JavaScript-libraries, you find the type declarations available on npm in the @types-organization. You can install these declarations from npm like any other package. Just use as a package name `@types/yourLibrary` when you call `npm install`.

12. Angular with TypeScript

Introduction

Google's popular Single Page Application (SPA) framework AngularJS has been completely re-written in TypeScript for version 2. With that version 2, the JS-suffix has been removed from the name, it's just Angular. The reason was that beside JavaScript also other languages, like for example TypeScript, can be used to build Angular applications.

The team at Google also switched to semantic versioning, which means that the version numbers of Angular will increase more frequently. But future versions will be backwards compatible with version 2. So, in this chapter we call it just Angular, but we mean version >=2.

Angular applications are built with components. You can nest these components into each other to build a full application. And of course, you can use TypeScript, which makes the development of Angular apps an awesome experience.

In this chapter, we start from scratch. You'll learn about the contents of a simple Hello world app. Then you learn how to display lists, how to create data bindings, how to connect to GitHub from your app and much more.

Before we begin where everything about programming starts (Hello world!) you read how to run the Angular samples of this book.

> **Note**
> You find the official Angular documentation on www.angular.io

Run the Angular Book Samples

All the Angular samples of this book are located in the folder *12* of the GitHub repository on https://github.com/thomasclaudiushuber/Getting-Started-with-TypeScript

All samples contain a *package.json*-file. Listing 12.1 shows the *package.json*-file of the Hello world-app. As you can see, it contains a `start`-script like you've used it already in chapter 9, "Modules". It has also different dependencies: To several angular packages, to SystemJS, and for development to the lite-server and to the concurrently-library.

```
{
  ...
  "scripts": {
    "start": "tsc && concurrently \"tsc -w\" \"lite-server\" "
  }, ...
  "dependencies": {
    "@angular/common": "~2.4.0",
    "@angular/compiler": "~2.4.0",
    "@angular/core": "~2.4.0",
    ...
    "systemjs": "0.19.40",
    ...
  },
  "devDependencies": {
    "concurrently": "^3.1.0",
    "lite-server": "^2.2.2"
  }, ...
}
```

Listing 12.1: 12\01_helloWorld\package.json

> **Note**
>
> As you can see, the angular-packages start with an @-character. The @-character says that this is an organization in npm. And only an organization can contain many sub-packages. So, Google created the @angular-organization to split up the angular framework into separate modules, like `@angular/core` or `@angular/compiler`. You've already seen another organization in this book: The @types-organization. We looked at it in chapter 11, "Declaration Files". The @types-organization contains all the packages with declaration files for popular JavaScript-libraries like lodash.

To start an application, you need to do two things: First you need to install the dependencies, and then you need to run the start script. That's it. To install the dependencies, you run this command on the command line:

```
npm install
```

As you know, this command downloads all the dependencies that you have defined in your *package.json*-file into a local *node_modules*-folder, including the developer dependencies.

With the dependencies installed, you can start and run the application by calling the `start`-script defined in the *package.json*-file from the command line with this command:

```
npm start
```

Pretty simple, isn't it? There's nothing new for you, you learned already about all of this in chapter 9, "Modules". Seems like you're already an experienced developer in this area.

Hello World in Angular

To get started with Angular, you can download the official quickstart-sample from GitHub: https://github.com/angular/quickstart. This quickstart-sample contains a lot of files that are great to start a real-world app. But for a simple application many of these files are not necessary. There are for example files for testing like *karma.conf.js* and *karma-test-shim.js*. But in this chapter, I want you to focus on the key parts of Angular: Components, Data Binding, Services, Dependency Injection etc.

Thus, all these files that are not required to build an application have been removed from all the book-samples. The Hello World-sample of this book sits in the folder *12\01_helloWorld*. It has the following files:
- *app/app.component.ts*
- *app/app.module.ts*
- *app/main.ts*
- *index.html*
- *package.json*
- *systemjs.config.js*
- *tsconfig.json*

You already know some of them, like for example the *package.json*-file. Now let's go through the contents of the other files. Let's start with the *app.component.ts*-file.

Listing 12.2 shows the contents of the *app.component.ts*-file. This file contains the component that is loaded on startup. At the top of the file you can see an import statement for the `Component`-decorator that is located in the `@angular/core`-module.

The file contains an `AppComponent`-class that has a `name`-property which is set to Thomas. The `AppComponent`-class is exported from this file with the `export`-keyword.

The `AppComponent`-class is decorated with the imported `Component`-decorator. An object is passed to that decorator that has a `selector`-property and a `template`-property. The `selector`-property defines the html-tag that you can use to reference this component. The `template`-property describes the user interface of the component. It's an html-snippet.

> **Note**
>
> The object passed to the `Component`-decorator is also known as a component's metadata.

But when you look closely, you can see that the template is referencing the `name`-property of the `AppComponent`-class by using that property inside of two opening and two closing curly braces. At runtime, this component displays the heading "Hello Thomas". That means the template of a component describes the UI, and that UI is connected to the component's class, which contains the logic of the component.

```
import { Component } from '@angular/core';

@Component({
  selector: 'my-app',
  template: `<h1>Hello {{name}}</h1>`
})
export class AppComponent {
  name: string = "Thomas";
}
```

Listing 12.2: *12\01_helloWorld\app\app.component.ts*

> **Note**
>
> An Angular component is a class that has a `Component`-decorator.

Listing 12.3 shows the *index.html*-file. In that file the `AppComponent` is loaded inside of the body. Note how the `my-app`-tag is used. This tag has been specified as a selector in listing 12.2.

```
<body>
  <my-app>Loading AppComponent content here ...</my-app>
</body>
```

Listing 12.3: 12\01_helloWorld\index.html

> **Note: Hyphen in selector**
>
> You should always put a hyphen in your component's selector, like we did with `my-app` in listing 12.2. Standard html elements will never contain a hyphen, this is described in the html-standard. So, when you put a hyphen into your component's selector, you can be sure that there's no overlapping today and also not tomorrow with any standard html element.

In Angular, a component belongs to an Angular module. An Angular module is a class that has the `NgModule`-decorator. This is an Angular specific concept to structure your code, it has nothing to do with TypeScript/ES2015 modules like described in chapter 9, "Modules".

Every Angular app has a root module. That root module is shown in listing 12.4. It's a class called `AppModule` that has an `NgModule`-decorator. As you can see, the root module imports another module, the `BrowserModule`. Note also that the `AppComponent` is declared as part of this root module in the declarations-array. When we introduce other components, we'll have additional declarations there.

The `AppComponent` is also defined as a bootstrap component. That means this component is fired up on start by the `AppModule`. But where is this "start" actually happening?

```
import { NgModule } from '@angular/core';
import { BrowserModule } from '@angular/platform-browser';
import { AppComponent } from './app.component';

@NgModule({
  imports: [BrowserModule],
  declarations: [AppComponent],
  bootstrap: [AppComponent]
})
export class AppModule { }
```

Listing 12.4: 12\01_helloWorld\app\app.module.ts

The start of the Angular app happens in the `main.ts`-file. Listing 12.5 shows the contents of this file. It imports the `plaformBrowserDynamic`-function and the `AppModule`. It calls the `plaformBrowserDynamic`-function that returns a platform reference, on which the `bootstrapModule`-function is called to bootstrap the `AppModule` from listing 12.4. Behind the scenes Angular will find the `AppComponent` as a bootstrap-component like defined in listing 12.4. Then Angular will load the `AppComponent` into the *index.html*-file where the `my-app`-tag has been specified (listing 12.3).

```
import { platformBrowserDynamic }
                    from '@angular/platform-browser-dynamic';
import { AppModule } from './app.module';

platformBrowserDynamic().bootstrapModule(AppModule);
```

Listing 12.5: 12\01_helloWorld\app\main.ts

> **Note**
> When you build a web app, the bootstrapping will always happen in the browser like in listing 12.5. But you can also build a desktop app with Angular and Electron, or a mobile app with Cordova, Ionic or even NativeScript. Then the bootstrapping won't happen in a browser, but in the specific environment that you've chosen.

Now the question is, who starts the *main.ts*-file, respectively the compiled *main.js*-file? When you look at the *index.html*-file in listing 12.6, you can see that the module loader SystemJS is set up. The configuration is located in a separated config-file called *systemjs.config.js*.

```
<head>
  ...
  <script src="systemjs.config.js"></script>
  <script>
    System.import('app').catch(function (err) { console.error(err); });
  </script>
</head>
```

Listing 12.6: 12\01_helloWorld\index.html

Listing 12.7 shows the important contents of the *systemjs.config.js*-file. As you can see, the *main.js*-file is defined as the main entry point for the app. Under the `map`-property the app is mapped to the *app*-folder. So, due to that mapping, the `System.import('app')` statement in listing 12.6 looks into the *app*-folder and finds the *main.js*-file there, as it is defined as an entry point in listing 12.7. The loaded *main.js*-file itself bootstraps our Angular application.

```
(function (global) {
  System.config({ ...
    map: {
      // our app is within the app folder
      app: 'app',
      ...
    }
    packages: {
      app: {
        main: './main.js', // defines the entry point for the app
        defaultExtension: 'js'
      }
      ...
```

Listing 12.7: 12\01_helloWorld\systemjs.config.js

That's how it works.

As you might have noticed in this section, Angular makes heavy use of decorators. You've seen the decorators `Component` and `NgModule` in action, and there are several others in the Angular framework. As Angular is using decorators, the `experimentalDecorators` compiler option is set to `true` in the *tsconfig.json*-file like shown in listing 12.8.

```
{
  "compilerOptions": {
    "target": "es5",
    "module": "commonjs",
    ...
    "experimentalDecorators": true,
    ...
  }
}
```

Listing 12.8: 12\01_helloWorld\tsconfig.json

Directives in Angular

A directive in Angular is something that extends standard html. The `AppComponent` of the previous section is for example a directive, as it has its own html-tag. We've specified `my-app` as a tag. That means the `AppComponent` extends standard html, so it's a directive.

Angular has three kinds of directives:
- Components
- Structural directives
- Attribute directives

As mentioned, components have their own, custom html tag. Structural directives are changing the DOM-tree by adding or removing elements. You'll learn about the structural directives `ngFor` and `ngIf` in this chapter. Attribute directives are changing the appearance or the behaviour of an element. In this chapter, you learn about the `ngModel`-directive that is used to create a two-way data binding.

Now let's use the structural directive `ngFor`.

Create Lists with ngFor

You can use the `ngFor`-directive to create a kind of for -loop in the html-template of your component. This is important when you want to create lists of elements. Let's look at how this works. The *friend.ts*-file shown in listing 12.9 defines the `Friend`-interface. It also creates an array of `Friend`-objects that is stored in the `FRIENDLIST`-variable. The `Friend`-interface and the array stored in the `FRIENDLIST`-variable are exported from the *friend.ts*-file.

```
export interface Friend {
    name: string;
    github: string
}

export let FRIENDLIST: Friend[] =
    [{ name: "Thomas", github: "thomasclaudiushuber" },
    { name: "Microsoft", github: "microsoft" },
    { name: "Angular Team", github: "angular" }]
```

Listing 12.9: *12\02_listsWithNgFor\app\friend.ts*

Listing 12.10 shows the *app.component.ts*-file that is importing the Friend-interface and the FRIENDLIST. The AppComponent-class has a friends-property that is initialized with the FRIENDLIST. It has also a selectedFriend-property and a method onFriendSelect that sets that selectedFriend-property to the value of the friend-parameter.

```
import { Friend, FRIENDLIST } from './friend';
import { Component } from '@angular/core';

@Component({
  selector: 'my-app',
  template: `...`
})
export class AppComponent {
  friends: Friend[] = FRIENDLIST;

  onFriendSelect(friend: Friend) {
    this.selectedFriend = friend;
  }

  selectedFriend: Friend;
}
```
Listing 12.10: 12\02_listsWithNgFor\app\app.component.ts

Listing 12.11 shows the template of the AppComponent. The ngFor-directive is used to loop over the friends in the friends-property. The ngFor-directive will create a li-element for each Friend-object in the friends-property. Inside of the li-element the name of the current friend is displayed with {{friend.name}}.

```
@Component({
  selector: 'my-app',
  template: `<h1>Select a friend</h1>
    <ul>
      <li *ngFor="let friend of friends"
          (click)="onFriendSelect(friend)">
            {{friend.name}}
      </li>
    </ul>`
})
export class AppComponent { ... }
```
Listing 12.11: 12\02_listsWithNgFor\app\app.component.ts

The `click`-event of the `li`-element in listing 12.11 is bound to the `onFriendSelect`-method of the `AppComponent`-class. That means when the `click`-event occurs, the `onFriendSelect`-method is called. The friend used for that `li`-element is passed to the `onFriendSelect`-method as an argument.

When you run the application, you see that for each friend a `li`-element is created. In figure 12.1 the friends Thomas, Microsoft and Angular Team are displayed. Exactly how we've specified these friends in the `FRIENDLIST`-variable of listing 12.9.

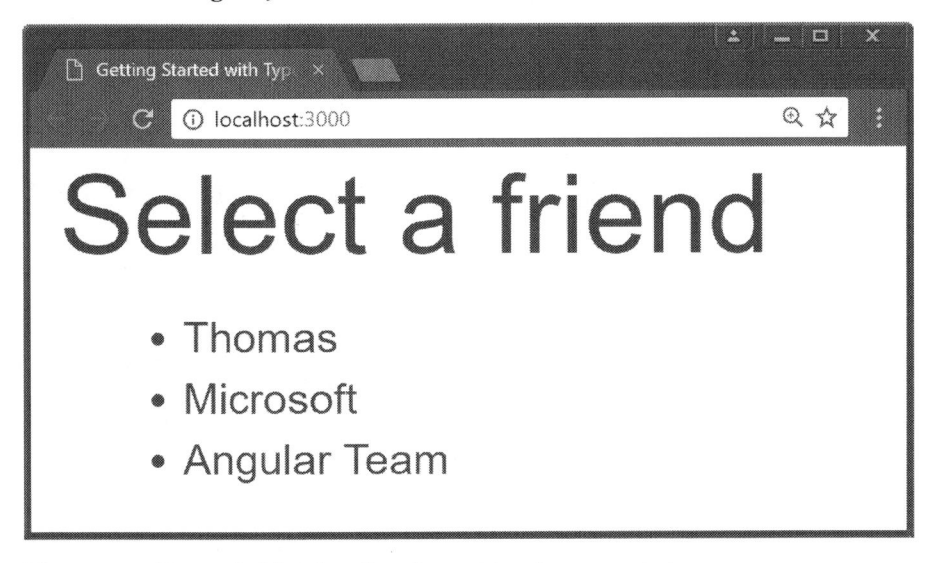

Figure 12.1: For each friend a <li>-element has been created.

When you select a friend in the list shown in figure 12.1, you cannot see the selection, but the `onFriendSelect`-method of the `AppComponent` was called. To be able to see the selection, we need to add some styling via CSS.

The metadata-object passed to the `Component`-decorator has a `styles`-property. It can contain an array of styles that are only valid for this specific component. In listing 12.12 this array contains just a single item, the CSS-class `isSelected`. The `isSelected`-class defines the value `bold` for the `font-weight`-property. On the `li`-element Angular's `class`-directive is used to set that `isSelected`-class. The `class`-directive is an attribute directive from Angular that allows you to set CSS-classes on elements based on an evaluated expression.

In listing 12.12 the expression checks if the friend used for the `li`-element is equal to the `selectedFriend`-property of the `AppComponent`. If that's the case, the `isSelected`-class is set on that `li`-element, else the `isSelected`-class is not set. This means the selected friend is displayed in bold.

```
@Component({
  selector: 'my-app',
  template: `<h1>Select a friend</h1>
    <ul>
      <li *ngFor="let friend of friends" style="cursor:pointer"
        [class.isSelected]="friend == selectedFriend"
          (click)="onFriendSelect(friend)">
            {{friend.name}}
      </li>
    </ul>`,
  styles: [`.isSelected{font-weight:bold;}`]
})
export class AppComponent { ... }
```

Listing 12.12: *12\02_listsWithNgFor\app\app.component.ts*

To make it clear that the user can select something, the `style`-attribute on the `li`-element in listing 12.12 changes the `cursor` to `pointer`, which displays a hand on windows when the item is hovered.

Figure 12.2 shows the application. The friend "Thomas" has been selected, now it's displayed in bold as the `isSelected`-class is set for that element.

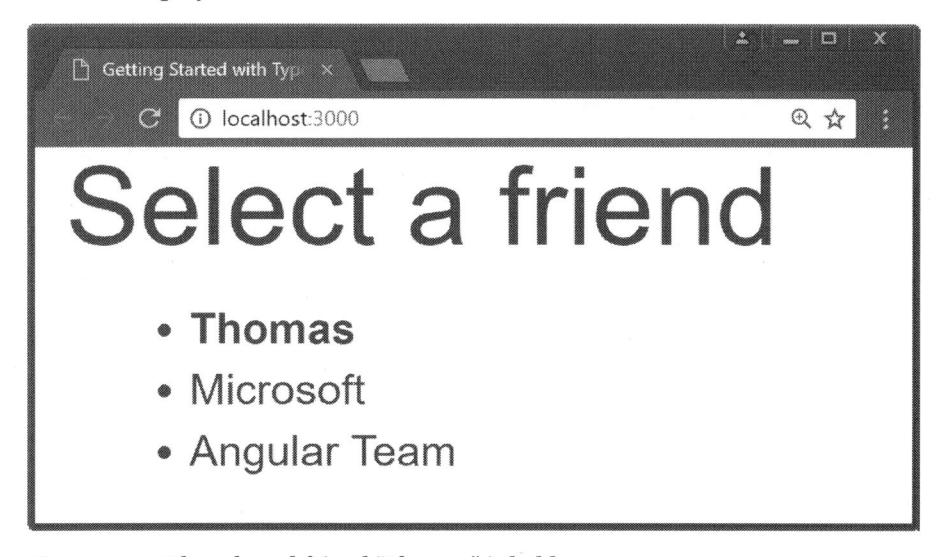

Figure 12.2: *The selected friend "Thomas" is bold*

Display Details with ngIf

The `ngIf`-directive is a structural directive that allows you to show html-elements based on a condition. Let's assume we want to show details of the selected friend. Listing 12.13 shows the adjusted template of the `AppComponent`. On a `div`-tag the `ngIf`-directive is used. If the `selectedFriend`-property of the `AppComponent` is not null, the `div`-element is displayed, else it's not displayed.

```
@Component({
  selector: 'my-app',
  template: `<h1>Select a friend</h1>
    <ul>
      ...
    </ul>
    <div *ngIf="selectedFriend != null">
      <div>
        <label>name:</label>
        <span>{{selectedFriend.name}}</span>
      </div>
      <div>
        <label>github:</label>
        <span>{{selectedFriend.github}}</span>
      </div>
    </div>`,
  styles: [`.isSelected{font-weight:bold;}`]
})
export class AppComponent {
  ...
  selectedFriend: Friend;
}
```

Listing 12.13: 12\03_displayDetailsWithNgIf\app\app.component.ts

Without selecting a friend, no details are visible. In figure 12.3 the friend Thomas is selected and the details appear. You can see the name of the selected friend and also the GitHub username.

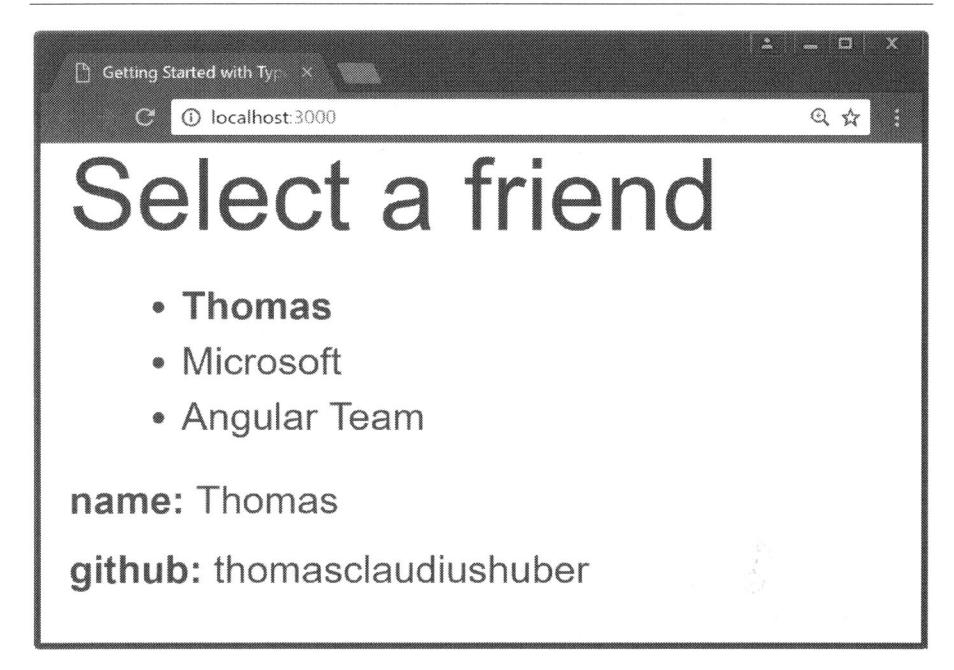

```
┌─────────────────────────────────────────────────┐
│ 📄 Getting Started with Typ  ×                  │
│   C  ⓘ localhost:3000                    ⊕ ☆   │
│                                                 │
│  Select a friend                                │
│                                                 │
│     • Thomas                                    │
│     • Microsoft                                 │
│     • Angular Team                              │
│                                                 │
│  name: Thomas                                   │
│  github: thomasclaudiushuber                    │
│                                                 │
└─────────────────────────────────────────────────┘
```

Figure 12.3: The details of the selected friend are displayed

> **Note**
> The `ngIf`-directive is a structural directive. It does not hide or show an element by using styles. Instead it adds or removes the complete element from the DOM-tree.

Data Binding in Angular

So far, you've already seen some data bindings in this chapter. The table below contains an overview:

Syntax	Usage
{{ }}	Show a property-value of the component-class in the template
[]	Bind an element-property in your template to a property of your component-class (one-way)
()	Bind an element-event in your template to a method of your component-class
[()]	Bind an element-property in your template to a property of your component-class (two-way).

For the two-way data binding you might have to think sometimes whether the syntax is ([]) or [()]. Just use the "banana in a box"-mnemonic to get the syntax right, then you know it's [()].

Add a Two-Way Data Binding

To use a two-way data binding, you have to add Angular's `FormsModule` to your `AppModule` like shown in listing 12.14.

```
import { HttpModule } from '@angular/http';
import { NgModule } from '@angular/core';
import { BrowserModule } from '@angular/platform-browser';
import { FormsModule } from '@angular/forms'

import { AppComponent } from './app.component';

@NgModule({
  imports: [BrowserModule, FormsModule],
  declarations: [AppComponent],
  bootstrap: [AppComponent]
})
export class AppModule { }
```
Listing 12.14: 12\04_twoWayBinding\app\app.module.ts

Now you can use the [()]-syntax with Angular's `ngModel`-directive that comes from the imported `FormsModule` of listing 12.14 to create a two-way data binding. Listing 12.15 shows an `input`-element that is bound two-way to the `name`-property of the `selectedFriend`.

```
@Component({
  selector: 'my-app',
  template: `...
    <div *ngIf="selectedFriend != null">
      <div>
        <label>name:</label>
        <input type="text" [(ngModel)]="selectedFriend.name">
      </div>
      ... })
export class AppComponent {
```
Listing 12.15: 12\04_twoWayBinding\app\app.component.ts

Angular's `ngModel`-directive updates the `value`-property of the `input`-element in listing 12.15 behind the scenes to the selected friend's name. And as we've created a two-way data binding in listing 12.15, the `name`-property of the selected friend is updated as well when the user is typing into that `input`-element and its `value`-property changes.

In figure 12.4, the name of the friend Thomas has been updated to Thomas Claudius. Note that the name is not only updated in the `input`-element. The `li`-element contains also the new name. The `li`-element updates after every change to the `input`-element.

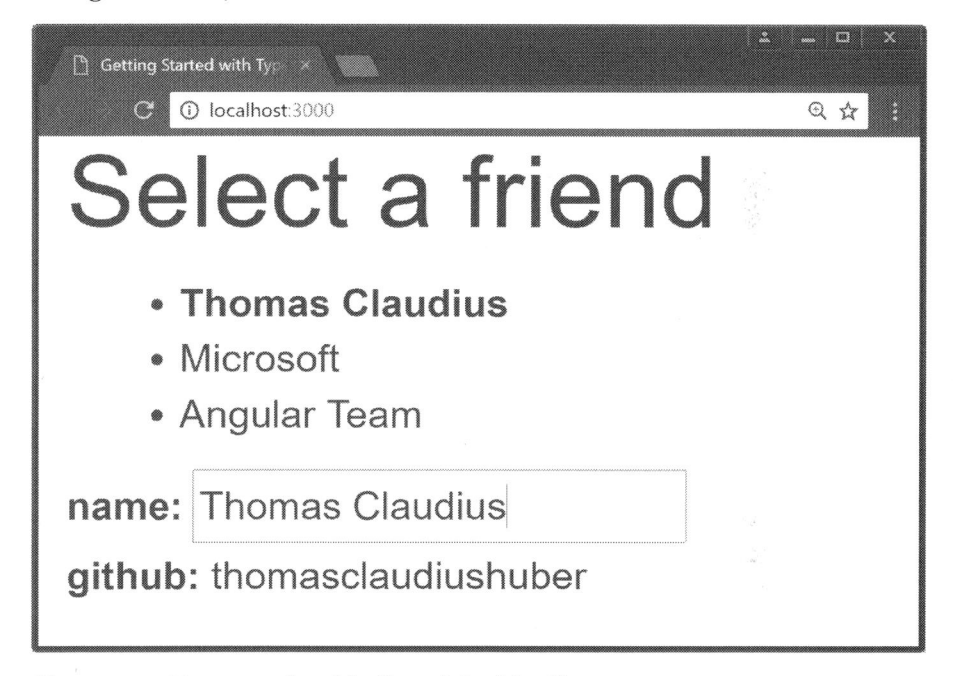

Figure 12.4: Two-way data binding of the friend's name.

Create a Friend Component

So far, we've coded everything into a single component, the `AppComponent`. But when you're building a bigger Angular app, it might get hard to maintain it if everything is just in a single component. And as Angular allows you to create multiple components and nest them, you should split your application up where it makes sense.

In the application that we've build so far, it makes for example sense to move the part that displays the details for a friend into a separate

FriendComponent. And that's exactly what we do in this section.

Listing 12.16 shows the AppComponent like we have created it. Now let's move the parts in bold to a separate FriendComponent.

```
@Component({
  selector: 'my-app',
  template: `...
    <div *ngIf="selectedFriend">
      <div>
        <label>name:</label>
        <input type="text" [(ngModel)]="selectedFriend.name">
      </div>
      <div>
        <label>github:</label>
        <span>{{selectedFriend.github}}</span>
      </div>
    </div>`, ... })
export class AppComponent { ... }
```

Listing 12.16: We move the parts in bold to a separate FriendComponent

First you need to create the file *friend.component.ts*. Then create a FriendComponent-class in that file that has a friend-property. Don't forget to add the export-keyword in front of the class like shown in listing 12.17.

```
import { Friend } from './friend';
import { Component } from '@angular/core';

@Component({
    selector: 'my-friend',
    template:`
    <div>
        <label>name:</label>
        <input type="text" [(ngModel)]="friend.name">
    </div>
    <div>
        <label>github:</label>
        <span>{{friend.github}}</span>
    </div>` })
export class FriendComponent {
    friend:Friend;
}
```

Listing 12.17: 12\05_createFriendComponent\app\friend.component.ts

As you can see in listing 12.17, the `FriendComponent`-class is decorated with Angular's `Component`-decorator. This makes the class an Angular component. The selector is set to `my-friend`. The template contains the code that was cut from the `AppComponent`-class in listing 12.16. The only thing that has been adjusted in the template are the bindings. The `FriendComponent`-class contains a `friend`-property, while the `AppComponent`-class has a `selectedFriend`-property. So, we need to bind to the `friend`-property, and not to the `selectedFriend`-property.

Now the `FriendComponent` is done. Nearly. We want to use it inside of the `AppComponent`, and we want to write to its `friend`-property with a one-way data binding. To make this work, we need to decorate the `friend`-property with Angular's `Input`-decorator like shown in listing 12.18. Note how this `Input`-decorator is also imported from `@angular/core`.

```typescript
import { Friend } from './friend';
import { Component, Input } from '@angular/core';

@Component({
    selector: 'my-friend',
    template:`...`
})
export class FriendComponent {
    @Input()
    friend:Friend;
}
```

Listing 12.18: 12\05_createFriendComponent\app\friend.component.ts

To be able to use the `FriendComponent` in the `AppComponent`, we need to declare it in the `AppModule` like shown in listing 12.19.

```typescript
import { FriendComponent } from './friend.component';
...

@NgModule({
  imports: [BrowserModule, FormsModule],
  declarations: [AppComponent, FriendComponent],
  bootstrap: [AppComponent]
})
export class AppModule { }
```

Listing 12.19: 12\05_createFriendComponent\app\app.module.ts

Now we can use the FriendComponent. Listing 12.20 shows the adjusted AppComponent that uses the FriendComponent with the tag my-friend like we have defined it as a selector on the FriendComponent. The friend-property of the FriendComponent is bound to the selectedFriend-property of the AppComponent. A one-way binding is used, as square brackets are around the friend-property. So, whenever the selectedFriend-property of the AppComponent changes, the friend-property of the FriendComponent is updated.

```
@Component({
  selector: 'my-app',
  template: `...
    <div *ngIf="selectedFriend">
      <my-friend [friend]="selectedFriend"></my-friend>
    </div>`,...
})
export class AppComponent {
  ...
  selectedFriend: Friend;
}
```

Listing 12.20: 12\05_createFriendComponent\app\app.component.ts

When you use the application, you don't see any difference. It looks and works exactly the same as before, as you can see in figure 12.5. When you select a friend like in figure 12.5, the details of that friend are displayed. But behind the scenes, we have structured our code into two Angular components, the AppComponent and the FriendComponent.

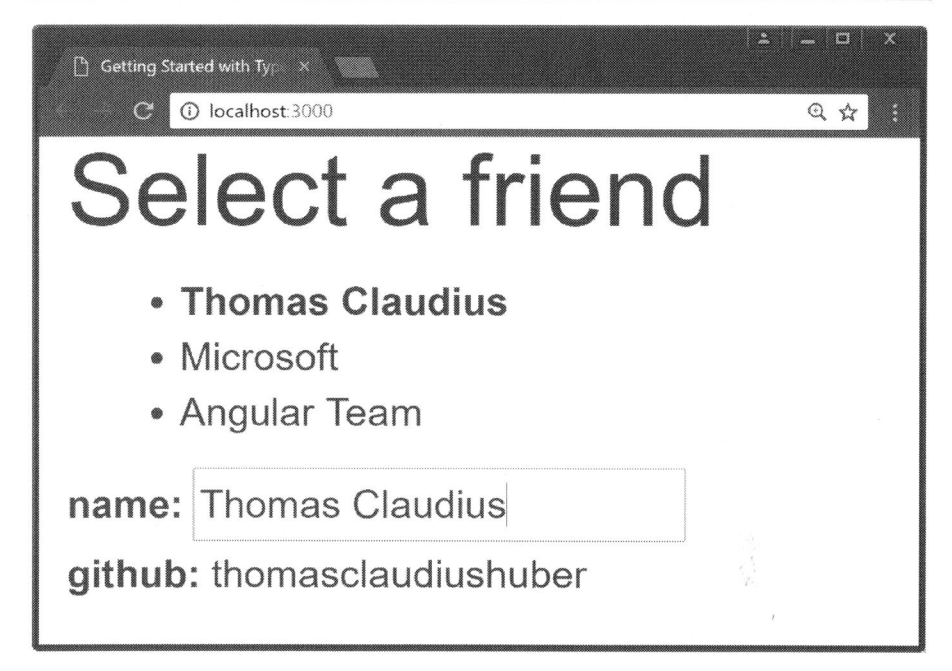

Figure 12.5: The details are displayed by the FriendComponent

Connect to GitHub via Http

To give our application a bit more value, we'll connect to GitHub in this section to display the GitHub repositories for the selected friend. Listing 12.21 shows the adjusted `FriendComponent` that has a new `githubRepos`-property of type `GithubRepo`. The `GithubRepo`-interface has the two properties `name` and `language`, both of type `string`.

```
export class FriendComponent {
    @Input()
    friend: Friend;
    ...
    githubRepos:GithubRepo[]
}
interface GithubRepo {
    name: string;
    language: string;
}
```

Listing 12.21: 12\06_connectToGithub\app\friend.component.ts

Listing 12.22 shows the html-table that has been added to the template of the `FriendComponent`. The `ngFor`-directive is used to create a `tr`-element for each `GithubRepo`-object in the `githubRepos`-property. The properties `name` and `language` of each `GithubRepo` are displayed in the html-table.

```
@Component({
    selector: 'my-friend',
    template: `...
    <h2>Github repos of {{friend.name}}</h2>
    <table>
        <tr>
           <th>Name</th>
           <th>Language</th>
        </tr>
        <tr *ngFor="let repo of githubRepos">
           <td>{{repo.name}}</td>
           <td>{{repo.language}}</td>
        </tr>
    </table>`
})
export class FriendComponent { ... }
```

Listing 12.22: *12\06_connectToGithub\app\friend.component.ts*

Now we need to load the repository information from GitHub. But how do we get that information from GitHub?

No worries, it's quite simple. GitHub as a nice Web API that returns the information about repositories as JSON. Here's the URL that returns an array with information about my public repositories: https://api.github.com/users/thomasclaudiushuber/repos. The returned array has an object for each repository. Each object itself has a lot of properties, and two of them are `name` and `language`, like we have defined them in our `GithubRepo`-interface in listing 12.21.

Listing 12.23 shows the structure of the JSON-file returned from GitHub with the important parts. Now we just need to make an http-call to the URL. Then we can fill the `githubRepos`-property of the `FriendComponent` with the results in form of a `GithubRepo`-array.

```
[{
  name: "EventHub.RestClientGenerator",
  language: "C#",
  ...
},
{
  name: "Getting-Started-with-TypeScript",
  language: "JavaScript",
  ...
}
]
```

Listing 12.23: The structure of the JSON-file returned from GitHub

To make http-requests, we need to import Angular's `HttpModule`. This import is done in the `AppModule` like shown in listing 12.24.

```
import { HttpModule } from '@angular/http';
...

@NgModule({
  imports: [BrowserModule, FormsModule, HttpModule],
  declarations: [AppComponent, FriendComponent],
  bootstrap: [AppComponent]
})
export class AppModule { }
```

Listing 12.24: 12\06_connectToGithub\app\app.module.ts

With the imported `HttpModule`, we can use the `Http`-class of that module in the `FriendComponent` to load the GitHub repositories for the selected friend.

In listing 12.25 the Http-class is imported. The constructor has a parameter property of type Http. But who passes that parameter to the constructor?

To answer this question, you need to think about who is calling the constructor of the FriendComponent-class. The constructor is called by Angular to create the FriendComponent, as it is used in the AppComponent's template with the my-friend-tag.

But does that mean that Angular is passing in an Http-object? Yes, exactly. Angular has integrated dependency injection support. By importing the HttpModule in listing 12.24, an Http-instance gets injected into your constructor if you have defined a parameter of that type. We have such a constructor parameter in the FriendComponent-class. That means at runtime Angular calls the constructor of the FriendComponent-class and passes in an Http-object. Great, so this works out of the box. Now we just need to use the Http-object stored in the http-property of the FriendComponent to make an http request to GitHub.

In the loadGithubRepos-method of listing 12.25 the get-method of the Http-object is called. Note how a template string is used for the URL that returns the JSON-array with the GitHub repositories. The github-property of the friend is used for the username-part in the URL. The get-method returns an Observable<Response>-object. The Observable-class comes from the Reactive Extensions library for JavaScript, or short rxjs. That library contains a map-function that is imported at the top of listing 12.25. This map-function is used on the Observable<Response>-object to map the JSON-result to a GithubRepo-array. By calling the subscribe-method, the request is executed and the returned GithubRepo-array is stored in the githubRepos-property of the FriendComponent. That's it! The logic to load the data is implemented, now we just need to call this loadGithubRepos-method somewhere.

> **Note**
>
> Look at the code in listing 12.25. There are a lot of arrow functions. As you know from chapter 8, "Functions", arrow functions capture this from the outer context. That's important when you look at the call of the subscribe-method: this is used to refer to the githubRepos-property of the FriendComponent-instance.

```
import { Http } from '@angular/http';
import 'rxjs/add/operator/map';
...

@Component(...)
export class FriendComponent {
    @Input()
    friend: Friend;

    constructor(private http: Http) { }

    loadGithubRepos() {
        return this.http.get(
           `https://api.github.com/users/${this.friend.github}/repos`)
            .map(res => res.json() as GithubRepo[])
            .subscribe(res => this.githubRepos = res);
    }

    githubRepos: GithubRepo[]
}
```

Listing 12.25: 12\06_connectToGithub\app\friend.component.ts

The `loadGithubRepos`-method of our `FriendComponent` should be called whenever the `friend`-property changes. Instead of adding a set-accessor for the `friend`-property, we can also implement Angular's `OnChanges`-interface like in listing 12.26. This interface defines a method `ngOnChanges` that is called whenever a data bound property changes. As the `friend`-property of the `FriendComponent` is data bound in the `AppComponent`, the `ngOnChanges`-method is a great place to call the `loadGithubRepos`-method of the `FriendComponent`.

```
import { Component, Input, OnChanges } from '@angular/core';
...

@Component(...)
export class FriendComponent implements OnChanges { ...
    ngOnChanges() {
        this.loadGithubRepos();
    } ...
}
```

Listing 12.26: 12\06_connectToGithub\app\friend.component.ts

Now we're done. We have implemented the `loadGithubRepos`-method that does the http call to GitHub, and we call that method in the `ngOnChanges`-method of listing 12.26. Time to run our little application.

When you select a friend, the GitHub repositories of that friend are displayed with name and language. In figure 12.6 the friend Thomas is selected. The GitHub repositories for the GitHub username thomasclaudiushuber are displayed at the bottom.

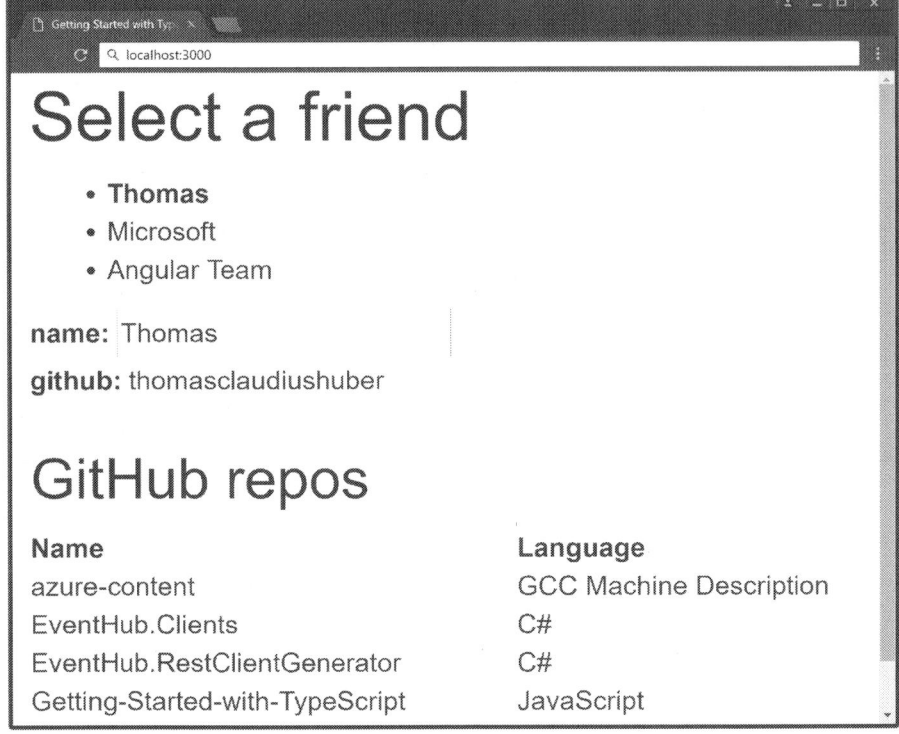

Figure 12.6: GitHub repositories are displayed for the selected friend.

Extract Http-logic into a Service

In the previous section, we've loaded the GitHub repos of a friend by executing a http-request directly in the FriendComponent. Listing 12.27 shows that full code.

```
export class FriendComponent implements OnChanges {
    @Input()
    friend: Friend;

    constructor(private http: Http) { }

    ngOnChanges() {
        this.loadGithubRepos();
    }

    loadGithubRepos() {
        return this.http.get(
            `https://api.github.com/users/${this.friend.github}/repos`)
            .map(res => res.json() as GithubRepo[])
            .subscribe(res => this.githubRepos = res);
    }

    githubRepos: GithubRepo[]
}
interface GithubRepo {
    name: string;
    language: string;
}
```

Listing 12.27: 12\06_connectToGithub\app\friend.component.ts

Instead of doing the http-request directly in the FriendComponent like shown in listing 12.27, you can do the request also in a separate service class that gets injected into the FriendComponent. This makes your code more maintainable and also simpler to test. In a test, you could pass a fake service to your FriendComponent that does not do real http-requests.

So, let's extract that http-request logic from the FriendComponent and let's put it into a separate service class that we call GithubService. Listing 12.28 shows that new GithubService-class that is placed in the file *github.service.ts*.

The `GithubService`-class of listing 12.28 has a parameter property in the constructor of type `Http`. As you know already, this `Http`-object gets injected by Angular. The class has a `loadGithubRepos`-method that has a `githubUser`-parameter of type `string`. The `loadGithubRepos`-method uses the value of that `githubUser`-parameter to build the URL. After the `http.get`-call the `map`-method is called to map the result to a `GithubRepo`-array.

```
import { Http } from '@angular/http';
import { Injectable } from '@angular/core'
import 'rxjs/add/operator/map';

@Injectable()
export class GithubService {
    constructor(private http: Http) { }
    loadGithubRepos(githubUser: string) {
        return this.http.get(
            `https://api.github.com/users/${githubUser}/repos`)
            .map(res => res.json() as GithubRepo[]);
    }
}
export interface GithubRepo {
    name: string;
    language: string;
}
```

Listing 12.28: *12\07_useGithubService\app\github.service.ts*

Note the `Injectable`-decorator that is set on the `GithubService`-class in listing 12.28. This `Injectable`-decorator makes the `GithubService`-class available for Angular's dependency injection. But before a `GithubService`-instance can be injected to the constructor of our `FriendComponent`, we need to add it like in listing 12.29 to the `providers`-array of the `AppModule`.

```
import { GithubService } from './github.service';
...
@NgModule({
  imports: [BrowserModule, FormsModule, HttpModule],
  declarations: [AppComponent, FriendComponent],
  bootstrap: [AppComponent],
  providers: [GithubService]
})
export class AppModule { }
```

Listing 12.29: *12\07_useGithubService\app\app.module.ts*

With the `GithubService`-class registered in the `AppModule`, we can add a constructor-parameter of that type to the `FriendComponent`. Listing 12.30 shows this. A parameter property is used to store the received `GithubService`-instance in the `githubService`-property. Angular will inject this dependency when it creates the `FriendComponent`.

The `loadGithubRepos`-method is now using the `githubService`. It calls its `loadGithubRepos`-method and passes in the value of the `github`-property of the current friend. The `github`-property contains the GitHub username. On the result, the `subscribe`-method is called. The received `GithubRepo`-array is stored in the `githubRepos`-property of the `FriendComponent`.

When you run the application, it works as before. The GitHub repositories are displayed for the selected friend. But now we don't have any http-calls coded directly into our little `FriendComponent` of listing 12.30. That's good for maintainability and for testability.

```typescript
import { GithubService, GithubRepo } from './github.service';
...

@Component(...)
export class FriendComponent implements OnChanges {
    @Input()
    friend: Friend;

    constructor(private githubService: GithubService) { }

    ngOnChanges() {
        this.loadGithubRepos();
    }

    loadGithubRepos() {
        return this.githubService.loadGithubRepos(this.friend.github)
            .subscribe(res => this.githubRepos = res);
    }

    githubRepos: GithubRepo[]
}
```

Listing 12.30: 12\07_useGithubService\app\friend.component.ts

Summary

You got a little introduction into Google's popular Angular framework in this chapter. An Angular application consists of different components that are nested.

An Angular component is a class with a `Component`-decorator. The `Component`-decorator is used to define metadata that has at least a selector and a template. The selector is the html-tag that is used to instantiate that component. The template contains an html-snippet that describes the user interface of the component.

The template and the component-class can be connected via data binding. You learned in this chapter how to display values with `{{}}`, how to bind a property with `[]`, how to bind a property two-way with `[()]`, and how to bind an event to a method of your component-class with `()`.

When you look from a TypeScript point-of-view at this chapter, you've done a lot: You've created classes with methods, constructors and parameter properties. You imported modules, exported your component classes, you've used decorators like `Component`, `Input` or `Injectable` and much more. So, you see, all your TypeScript-knowledge that you gained by reading this book can be used to build web applications with Angular. And not only Angular, you can use TypeScript for every JavaScript-based application, as it compiles down to plain JavaScript.

Thanks for buying and reading this book. I hope you enjoyed it!

If you have any questions about the book, or if you have any feedback, recommendations or corrections, please don't hesitate to reach out to me:

Email: thomas@thomasclaudiushuber.com

Twitter: @thomasclaudiush

Thanks, and happy coding! ☺
Thomas Claudius Huber

Index

.

.d.ts-file extension 138
.js.map file extension 36
.ts file extension 28

@

@angular/core module 146
@angular-organization 144
@Component (Angular) 146
@Injectable (Angular) 168
@Input (Angular) 159
@NgModule (Angular) 147
@types-organization 138

A

Abstract classes 78
Access modifiers 71
    private 71
    protected 71
    public 71
Accessors (Properties) 75
Aliases (Modules) 119
amd 110
Angular 143
    @Component 146
    @Injectable 168
    @Input 159
    @NgModule 147
    AppComponent 146
    AppModule 147
    bootstrapModule 148
    BrowserModule 147
    Component 133
    Data binding 155
    Dependency injection 164

Directives 150
Documentation 143
FormsModule 156
Hello world 145
Http 161
HttpModule 163
Multiple components 157
plaformBrowserDynamic 148
Root module 147
Run project 143
selector 146
Services 167
SystemJS Setup 148
template 146
Annotations (Decorators) 125
Anonymous function 94
any 51
AppComponent (Angular) 146
AppModule (Angular) 147
Array-class 47, 85
Arrays 46
Arrow functions 101
as-operator (Type Assertions) 53
async 103
Attribute directives (Angular) 150
Attributes (Decorators) 125
await 103

B

Base class constructor 78
Basic types
    any 51
    array 46
    boolean 41
    enums 49
    never 57
    null 58

number 43
string 44
tuples 49
undefined 58
void 57
Binding (Angular) 155
Block-scoped (Variables) 61
Book
    Download samples 16
    Feedback 17
    Run Angular projects 143
    Run samples 17
boolean 41
bootstrapModule (Angular) 148
Browser console 27
BrowserModule (Angular) 147

C

Chrome
    Developer tools 27
    Installation 24
class (Angular) 152
Classes 67
    abstract 78
    Access modifiers 71
    constructor 67, 72
    Decorators 129
    Generics 88
    Implement interface 70
    in ES2015 69
    Inheritance 77
    Parameter properties 72
    Readonly properties 73
    this 67
commonjs 110
Compile errors 29
Compile TypeScript 17, 28
Compiler options 31, 33
    declaration 140
    experimentalDecorators 126

module 110
noEmitOnError 30
noImplicitAny 34, 51
sourceMap 36
strictNullChecks 58
target 34
Component (Angular) 133, 146, 157
concurrently 113
Console (Browser) 27
Console (Visual Studio Code) 26
const (Variables) 61, 64
constraints (Generics) 89
constructor 67
    Base class 78
    Parameter properties 72
    Parameters 79
Cordova 12, 148
Create object (new) 68
CSS 152

D

d.ts file extension (Declarations) 138
Data binding (Angular) 155
Debugging 35
Declaration files (.d.ts) 135
    Install from npm 137
declaration-option 140
declare 137
Decorators 125
    Component (Angular) 146
    for Classes 129
    for Properties 127
    Injectable (Angular) 168
    Input (Angular) 159
    ngModule (Angular) 147
    Targets of 126
Default export (Modules) 120
Default values (Functions) 95
defaultJSExtensions (SystemJS) 116
Dependency injection (Angular) 164

Destructuring
    Arrays 83
    Objects 81
Developer tools (Chrome) 27
Directives (Angular) 150

E

ECMA 12
ECMAScript (ES) 12
Electron 12, 148
Enums 49
Errors (compilation) 29
ES (ECMAScript) 12
ES2015 69
    Arrow functions 103
    Classes 69
    Destructuring 81
    for-of-loop 32
    Module format 110
    Modules 107
    Template strings 44
ES2017 104
ES5 68
experimentalDecorators-option 126
export (Modules) 108
    Alias 119
    Classes 108
    default 120
    Functions 121
    Variables 121

F

File extensions
    .d.ts (Declarations) 138
    .js.map (Mappings) 36
    .ts (TypeScript) 28
for-in-loop 48
FormsModule (Angular) 156
for-of-loop 47

FriendComponent 158
Functions 93
    Adding types 94
    and this 99
    Arrow functions 101
    as Parameters 97
    async/await 103
    Default values 95
    Generics 86
    Interfaces for 98
    Optional parameters 94
    Rest parameters (...) 96
    Types in JavaScript 93
Function-scoped (Variables) 61

G

-g parameter (npm) 22
Generics 85
    Array-class 85
    Classes 88
    Constraints 89
    Functions 86
    Interfaces 87
    Multipe parameters 91
get (Property) 75
getElementById 54
GitHub access via Http 161
Google Chrome
    Developer tools 27
    Installation 24
Gulp 38

H

HTMLElement 54
HTMLInputElement 54
html-tag 146
Http 161
HttpModule (Angular) 163

I

import (Modules).............................. 108
    Alias 120
Inference (Type) 42
Inheritance 77
Injectable (Angular) 168
Input (Angular) 159
Install (npm).............................. 17, 117
Install TypeScript (npm)..................... 22
instanceof... 80
Instantiate (new) 68
Integrated Terminal 26
Interfaces.. 65
    for Functions 98
    Generics 87
    Implementation 70
    Usage.. 29
Ionic 148

J

JavaScript.. 12
    Migrate to TypeScript..................... 29
    Run code 25
    Standards (ECMA) 12
    Use a library 135
js.map file extension.......................... 36
JSX.. 54

L

let (Variables) 61
lite-server 113
LTS 21

M

map file extension 36
map-function (rxjs) 164
Modifiers (Class access) 71

Module Loader 109
    SystemJS...................................... 111
module-option 110
Modules 107
    Aliases 119
    Default exports............................ 120
    export 108
    Export functions 121
    Export multiple types 117
    Export variables........................... 121
    Formats 110
    import... 108
    Import multiple types.................. 118

N

Named function 93
Namespaces...................................... 107
NativeScript 148
never.. 57
new (create object)............................ 68
ngFor (Angular) 150
ngIf (Angular) 154
ngModel (Angular) 157
NgModule decorator (Angular)......... 147
Node Package Manager (npm) ... 21, 111
Node.js... 21
noEmitOnError-option 30
noImplicitAny............................. 34, 51
Nominal typing 70
npm.. 21, 111
    Declaration files........................... 137
    -g parameter................................. 22
    init 112
    install 17, 117
    Organizations (@)........................ 144
    --save parameter 113
    --save-dev parameter 114
    start 17, 114
null 58
number 43

O

Object oriented 65
Observable (rxjs) 164
Optional parameters 94
Optional properties 66, 67

P

package.json
    Create config 111
    Install dependencies 117
Parameter properties 72
Parameters
    Default values 95
    for constructor 79
    Optional 94
    Rest (…) 96
plaformBrowserDynamic (Angular) .. 148
Polyfill 105
private 71
Properties
    Accessors 75
    Decorators 127
    Optional 66, 67
    Parameter properties 72
    readonly 73
    static 76
protected 71
public 71

R

React 12
Reactive Extensions (rxjs) 164
Readonly properties 73
Reflect-metadata 131
Rest parameters (…) 96
Run (Your Application) 117
rxjs (Reactive Extensions) 164

S

Samples
    Download 16
    Run 17
    Run Angular projects 143
--save parameter (npm) 113
--save-dev parameter (npm) 114
script-element 26, 116
selector (Angular) 146
    why with hyphen 147
set (Property) 75
sourceMap (tsconfig.json) 36
start (npm) 17, 114
Start (Your Application) 117
Statement completion 30
static 76
strictNullChecks-option 58
string 44
Structural directives (Angular) 150
    ngFor 150
    ngIf 154
Structural typing 70
styles (Angular) 152
Styling 152
subscribe 164
super (base constructor) 78
system 110
System.import 116
SystemJS 111
    Setup 115
    with Angular 148
SystemJS.config 116

T

-t parameter (tsc) 32
template (Angular) 146
Template strings 44
Terminal (Visual Studio Code) 26
this 67, 99, 102

ts file extension	28	TypeScript Compiler	
tsc	17, 28	declaration-option	140
tsconfig.json	33	experimentalDecorators-option	126
declaration	140	--init argument	33
experimentalDecorators	126	module-option	110
module	110	noEmitOnError-option	30
noEmitOnError	30	noImplicitAny-option	51
noImplicitAny	34, 51	options	31
sourceMap	36	sourceMap-option	36
strictNullChecks	58	strictNullChecks-option	58
target	34	-t parameter	32
Tuples	49	tsconfig.json	33
Two-way Binding (Angular)	156	-w parameter	28
Type assertions	53		
Type checking	80	**U**	
Type compatibility	70		
Type declarations (.d.ts)	137	umd	110
Type inference	42	undefined	58
TypeScript		Union types	55
Advantages of	15		
and Angular	143	**V**	
Classes	67		
Compile	17, 28	V8 (JavaScript engine)	21
Compiler	28	var (Variables)	61
Debugging	35	Variables	
Declaration files	137	const	64
Declare variables	61	function- vs. block-scoped	61
Decorators	125	let	61
Destructuring	81	var	61
Documentation	25	Visual Studio Code	23
Functions	93	hide .js-files	37
Generics	85	Integrated Terminal	26
Installation	22	void	57
Interfaces	65		
Modules	107	**W**	
Namespaces	107		
Type compatibility	70	-w parameter (tsc)	28
Type inference	42	WebStorm	23

Made in the USA
Columbia, SC
05 March 2018